Audience Responses to Real Media Violence

Audience Responses to Real Media Violence

The Knockout Game

Mary Grace Antony

LEXINGTON BOOKS
Lanham • Boulder • New York • London

Published by Lexington Books
An imprint of The Rowman & Littlefield Publishing Group, Inc.
4501 Forbes Boulevard, Suite 200, Lanham, Maryland 20706
www.rowman.com

Unit A, Whitacre Mews, 26-34 Stannary Street, London SE11 4AB

British Library Cataloguing in Publication Information Available

Library of Congress Cataloging-in-Publication Data

Antony, Mary Grace.
Audience responses to real media violence : the knockout game / Mary Grace Antony.
pages cm
Includes bibliographical references and index.
ISBN 978-0-7391-9611-3 (cloth : alk. paper) -- ISBN 978-0-7391-9612-0 (electronic)
1. Violence in mass media--Psychological aspects. 2. Violence--Psychological aspects. 3. Internet
videos--Psychological aspects. 4. Audiences--Psychology. 5. Mass media--Audiences. I. Title.
P96.V5A58 2015
303.6--dc23
2014047069

Printed in the United States of America

Contents

Acknowledgments

I owe a debt of gratitude to several people without whose support, guidance, and patience this project would not exist. This book is based on my doctoral dissertation research, and I am deeply grateful to my faculty advisor and committee chair, Dr. Rick W. Busselle, for his mentorship and support. Sincere thanks are also due to the faculty who served on my doctoral research committee: Dr. Jeffery C. Peterson, Dr. Mary Beth Oliver, and Dr. Changmin Yan. Their insightful comments and suggestions enabled me to develop and refine this project over the course of its progress.

A special thank you to Dr. Ryan J. Thomas, who co-authored an earlier draft of chapter 5 that was presented at the National Communication Association's 2011 annual convention.

I extend heartfelt love and gratitude to my family for their unconditional love, support, optimism, and encouragement through this endeavor. Specifically, my husband Tony, mother Marie, brother Mathew, and Cocoa.

Finally, a special word of appreciation for my friends at Lexington Books, without whom this publication would not exist. Alison Pavan and Emily Frazzette were a joy to work with, and their prompt correspondence and feedback (coupled with valuable feedback from the anonymous reviewer) facilitated a smooth transition from proposal to final manuscript.

I

How We Respond to Media Violence

"TV violence doesn't bleed. There are lots of shootouts and fist fights, but amazingly no one gets seriously hurt. TV rarely shows the consequences of violence" (Osborn 1993).

These words, uttered by journalist and media literacy commentator Barbara Osborn in the early 1990s are still disturbingly applicable to the vast majority of media violence representations today, whether crime drama series, action blockbuster movies, or graphic video games. Think about it. When was the last time you watched the realistic outcome of a hero's battle against evil that was not fundamentally manipulated by slick post-production visual effects and an awe-inspiring soundtrack? Can you remember the last TV show or movie that showed a victim's prolonged and agonizing recovery following the protagonist's brutal assault? In fact, some interactive formats—particularly video game genres that emphasize combat and deviant contexts—encourage and reward vicious sustained attacks on already weakened individuals. Players of these games are embedded in interactive scenarios where violence against aliens, zombies, monsters, and even fellow humans, is integral to their characters' performance and success.

Most of us have heard the familiar arguments linking violent entertainment media to hostile thoughts and aggressive imitative behavior. We frequently hear chilling stories about mentally disturbed young adults who carry out horrific school shootings and massacre innocent bystanders, only to eventually learn that many of these individuals had a disproportionate appetite for graphic media violence. Events such as these periodically revive tired old debates about the negative effects of video games and explicit media violence on impressionable young minds. And although these may well be valid concerns, it is not my intent to address behavioral outcomes here.

Instead, let us consider another effect of prolonged exposure to media violence: the diminished capacity to *feel* for its victims. Empathy is a hallmark characteristic that distinguishes us from other living beings, making us fundamentally human. Our ability to (figuratively) place ourselves in another's shoes provides the foundation for some of human-kind's most admirable qualities: cooperation, compassion, democracy, and justice, to name a few. So can exposure to media violence impact empathy? Sure. When we consistently experience media narratives that privilege a protagonist's perspective over that of other characters, and endorse attacks and crimes that this protagonist commits against others, we are likely to disregard the outcomes of violence. As Osborn concludes, "Perhaps the most chilling aspect of the media's portrayal of violence is that when people are killed, they simply disappear. No one mourns their death. Their lives are unimportant" (1993). We may briefly mourn the loss of a likeable sidekick or love interest, but the narrative motivates us to shake off this gloom and forge ahead beside our valiant hero—as, for instance, in the acclaimed blockbuster *The Hunger Games* trilogy.

However, as our media contexts become increasingly sophisticated and interactive, it is more important than ever to critically examine the cognitive and attitudinal effects of viewing media violence. In particular, the preponderance of "real" media genres and user-generated content has blurred the lines between traditional media fiction and the real world. Today's average media user is barraged with a range of content on multiple media platforms, from the 24/7 news cycle, to frequent Facebook updates, targeted spam mail, and periodic celebrity musings on Twitter. It has also never been easier to create media content. User-friendly interfaces, apps, and video-sharing websites like YouTube allow for the quick production and mass distribution of all manner of content: from the purely diversionary (consider cats drinking out of kitchen faucets), to the utilitarian (such as an online tutorial on how to impress the boss), to the expository—including brutal online footage of real-life attacks on victims. In the midst of this media melee, have our responses to media violence altered in any significant ways? And more importantly, how do we respond to *real* media violence? Is there a qualitative difference in our cognitive and affective responses to the victims of real versus fictional assaults? These are the questions that we shall consider in the following chapters as we examine the under-explored but alarmingly ubiquitous genre of real media violence.

Before we tackle these specific questions, however, it behooves us to review prior scholarship on affective responses to media violence—and empathy, in particular. This first section lays the necessary groundwork by outlining the nature and scope of contemporary real media violence and then identifying some relevant theoretical concepts.

Chapter 1 describes a recent sinister social trend that has made news headlines, colloquially referred to as the Knockout Game. These unsettling random attacks were recorded on smartphones and later posted online, and constitute a prime example of unfiltered raw violence that captures vicious—and sometimes lethal—attacks on unsuspecting victims. As an emerging media format that has received very little scholarly attention, Knockout Game videos are an excellent means to investigate affective and cognitive responses to real media violence.

Chapter 2 provides an overview of how we form emotional relationships with media characters. We learn how narratives contain cues that encourage us to form positive dispositions toward some characters and negative dispositions toward others. These dispositions in turn influence the nature of our empathic responses toward media characters.

Finally, chapter 3 explains how we rely on creative cognitive coping mechanisms to rationalize media violence, and thus enhance our overall enjoyment. I specifically focus on the utility of moral disengagement, as it applies to liked media characters, as a mechanism that allows us to underplay and ultimately enjoy media violence.

Following this, part II describes a series of original research projects that investigate how audiences respond to real media violence.

ONE

When Violence is Real, Not Reel

The video begins serenely enough. The pixelated and shaky image eventually settles to reveal an old man dozing on a bus that is almost empty. He does not notice the two adolescent boys who approach him, but is rudely awakened when they suddenly set on him with vicious kicks and punches. Stunned, the elderly passenger struggles to his feet, raising his arms to ward off the blows and trying to back away. But the punches keep coming. He staggers toward the nearest exit with the aggressive teenagers in hot pursuit, and briefly hesitates before jumping from the moving vehicle to escape his assailants. A third unseen assailant captures the entire attack on his cellphone and later posts the video online. The entire video is barely twenty seconds long.

It is difficult to initially determine exactly what is happening in this next video as the camera pans back and forth, zooming in and out a few times. But the blurry image finally resolves to depict an adolescent boy facing the camera. His gaze is averted because he is staring at the floor, deliberately avoiding looking directly into the camera. Despite the poor image resolution, purple bruises are evident on the boy's face and neck. The camera pans down to reveal that his hands and feet are tied with cord, and then tilts up to briefly focus on his downcast face again. Then an off-screen hand reaches into the frame and pulls the hood of his sweater over his head, tugging the strings so that it tightens and renders him blindfolded. Suddenly, an arm swings into view and punches the victim's head hard. He reels backward from the force of the impact, and then another arm lashes into him from the other side. Blow after heavy blow rain down on his torso and head. The video is approximately thirty-five seconds in duration.

The third video is clearer than the other two, and the grainy camera image focuses to reveal a dimly lit street. It is late and there is no traffic apart from a distant approaching speck. A figure dressed in dark clothes lurks in the foreground, his features hidden by a black hoodie. As the faraway speck approaches, we see that it is a cyclist speeding down the sloping road toward an intersection. He is in a hurry to get someplace and is now almost parallel with the pedestrian. Then without warning, the hooded man suddenly lashes out at the rider, catching him under the chin with a swift right hook. The cyclist is caught completely unaware. His momentum, coupled with the force of the assailant's blow, propel him backwards off his vehicle to the street. The camera briefly zooms in on the cyclist's dazed and disoriented expression before fading out. The entire video is just over seven seconds long.

These videos are a far cry from artificial, glamorized, and graphic violence that we often encounter in blockbuster Hollywood narratives and slick primetime television shows. They are cellphone footage of real attacks on everyday real people that were harvested from a simple You-Tube search. Although we are doubtless familiar with a plethora of media violence genres—from explosive action extravaganzas to futuristic sci-fi, slasher horrors, spine-tingling thrillers, and gorgeous fantasy sagas—videos such as those described above constitute a radically different type of media violence. They are indicative of the extremely unsettling yet emerging abundance of real violent media content online.

This particular subgenre demonstrates some characteristic features that distinguish it from other mediated portrayals of real violence. First, the content consists of raw and unfiltered footage of a real attack on an incapacitated or unsuspecting victim. Characterized by a random unpredictability that defies apparent reason or motive, vicious assaults are perpetrated against vulnerable victims who are typically caught completely unawares. The nature of the attack ranges in intensity from a single harsh blow to sustained and severe beatings, with sometimes lethal consequences. The attacks themselves are typically recorded by one of the assailants on a smartphone or other portable electronic device and posted online shortly thereafter. This media violence genre has existed in some form or another for the last fifteen years. In the early 2000s, Britain was witness to a spate of these videos. The press colloquially labeled them "happy slapping" videos, as in this report:

> In one video clip, labeled Bitch Slap, a youth approaches a woman at a bus stop and punches her in the face. In another, Knockout Punch, a group of boys wearing uniforms are shown leading another boy across an unidentified school playground before flooring him with a single blow to the head. . . . Welcome to the disturbing world of the "happy slappers"—a youth craze in which groups of teenagers armed with camera phones slap or mug unsuspecting children or passersby while capturing the attacks on 3g technology. (Honigsbaum 2005)

The victims were average folks going about their daily routine, and typically hailed from vulnerable categories, such as women, young children, and the elderly. Much like a natural disaster that descends without warning leaving devastation in its wake, vicious and belligerent adolescents set upon them in the least likely locations—on sidewalks, in residential areas, in subway stations, at the grocery store—and at any time of day. As the gang inflicted the cruel attack on its unsuspecting prey, one member always stood to the side, recording the event on a smartphone and later distributing the humiliating footage online. Child psychologists, journalists, and law enforcement authorities puzzled to explain this perplexingly randomized aggression, with many concluding that it was an unfortunate manifestation of extreme and sadistic bullying. "Happy slapping," it was hoped, was an alarming violent trend that would eventually dwindle and disappear. Yet that did not happen.

In recent months, we have witnessed a resurgence of the sinister fad, this time in the United States. It now goes by a new moniker: the Knockout Game. Yet the symptoms are identical. An unsuspecting and innocent victim is brutally set upon by aggressive youths, the random assault is recorded on a smartphone or similar electronic device and then posted online. In rare instances, the act of recording ultimately proves to be the assailants' undoing, and these videos have sometimes enabled authorities to identify and incriminate the attackers (Buckley, November 22, 2013). But such instances are few and far between. More often than not, the aggressors escape and later gleefully disseminate their digital "trophy" online. Some allege that recent assaults imply a disturbing racial motive, and argue that Knockout hoodlums target and attack victims from minority groups. Such was the case of a Texas youth who viciously assaulted an elderly African American man (Jonsson, December 27, 2013). Yet Knockout Games persist, in urban and rural contexts alike, as innocent victims are targeted and assailed by belligerent hoodlums.

Some commentators have drawn parallels between the Knockout Game and its precedent "happy slapping." One columnist suggests that the trend is an entrenched and recurring social pattern of young discontents enacting brutality on innocent victims, comparing Knockout Game perpetrators to the violent delinquents in Stanley Kubrick's classic *A Clockwork Orange* (Demby, November 27, 2013). Yet I am inclined to disagree with this analogy. Although both cases may prompt familiar concerns about media violence, "happy slapping" and Knockout Game videos are drastically different from fictional media violence representations in some important regards. First, the former imply an imitative behavioral manifestation stemming from violent media consumption—as opposed to the primarily passive viewership that characterizes most media audiences. While many of us are unlikely to respond to violent content beyond temporary physiological arousal during the viewing experience and (perhaps) post-viewing reflection, these young attackers are quite different from mainstream consumers. Watching media violence may actually spur and motivate them to commit real-world acts of aggression, as proven in a renowned series of experiments more than half a century ago that demonstrated the relationship between media violence and imitative aggression (Bandura 1965). Some law-enforcement officers even worry that the chaos may thrive upon itself as existing Knockout Game videos online inspire copycat crimes and further violence (Rossen and Patel, November 25, 2013).

A second feature that distinguishes Knockout Game videos from fictional media violence is the existence of the videos themselves. The very fact that these perpetrators record and post footage of their assaults online for mass display suggests a particularly sadistic intent. In other words, it is not enough for these young criminals to solely indulge their deviant inclinations in the act of violence. Instead, the video becomes a means by which they can later re-live and re-experience the attack ad nauseam. Furthermore, the act of uploading videos of the attacks to public virtual forums shifts these individuals from mere consumers of media violence to producers in their own right. Their content now competes with the diversity of other violent media already available to consumers . . . with one important difference. Unlike fictional media violence, these videos feature real attacks on real people. And a simple YouTube search using the keywords "knockout game" results in a range of search results, the popularity of which are evidenced by a staggering number of total views. For instance, the following videos appear on the very first page of search results: "Teen Playing the Knockout Game Gets Shot Twice by Victim" (3,032,963 views); "Knockout Game Gets Slammed on his Head" (47,011 views); "Knockout Game gets teen shot!" (1,826,089 views); "Knockout game: Large group of black thugs commit a premeditated attack against two men" (18,206 views); and "Knockout Game Death: England" (3,121 views). Although it is not possible to differentiate between first-time viewers versus repetitive views, or identify exactly how many viewers watched these videos solely for sadistic pleasure, the extremely high numbers demonstrate that these videos have been viewed by mass audiences.

Most research suggests that we enjoy watching entertainment media violence by relying on cognitive coping mechanisms. In other words, we can remind ourselves that we are watching a fictional representation enacted by actors and professional stunts-persons instead of real events. Therefore, no matter how intense or graphic the violence, we manage to enjoy it by assuring ourselves that it did not really happen. In doing so, we engage with the violence on a superficial level as spectators. Yet researchers warn that accumulated violent media viewing can desensitize audiences over time, increasing our appetites for ever more graphic portrayals while simultaneously diminishing our ability to empathize with victims of violence (Bandura 1999; 2002; 2007). In other words, as we get more accustomed to intensifying gratuitous displays of violence, our tolerance levels rise and this sets the stage for ever-increasing explicit and graphic violent content. Some might argue that the very labels *"happy slapping"* and Knockout *Game* suggest an already unsettling level of desensitization to violence among the perpetrators, indicating that they already regard these vicious attacks as amusing and funny. Accompanying descriptions and comments posted to these videos typically celebrate the attack and its aftermath, directing viewers' attention to specific details such as, "Watch the guy in the brown hoodie—his facial expression is epic." Interestingly, an etymological investigation into the origins of the term "slaphappy" reveal that it refers to a mental state in which one is "dazed or stupefied as if by a series of blows to the head" (Oxford Dictionaries 2014). In a cruel linguistic twist, the figurative expression portends its current literal manifestation (albeit through reversed verbiage) in "happy slapping" videos where victims are indeed the target of several repeated blows.

The popularity of reality TV has facilitated an unprecedented infatuation with cellphone videos and user-generated content, as evidenced by the success of video-sharing websites such as YouTube. Increasingly compact technological devices, such as smartphones, mini tablets, and affordable surveillance equipment, allow anyone to become an amateur filmmaker. Yet, particularly with regard to violence, online user-generated videos seldom receive the rigorous attention and editing that we see in traditional mainstream content. Run a quick online search using the right keywords and you will quickly discover a range of audiovisual material, ranging in intensity from harmless slapstick violence to gruesome and graphic gore. The majority of this content is not subject to scrutiny or careful decision making as to whether or not it should be made available for public viewing. Indeed, most of the time, it does not received any scrutiny at all. Websites such as YouTube typically rely on a process of community policing, where the onus rests on users to indicate or "flag" certain content as inappropriate. If enough viewers complain, an objectionable video may be removed. The prevalence and nature of violent videos on public websites thus depends entirely on who exactly watches them. If most viewers and visitors to the website neither mind nor report the graphic content, the video is not "pulled" off the website. As a result, audiences today are frequently confronted with a glut of unfiltered images of real people in violent situations, as well as those in which real victims are subjected to pain and suffering. Examples include raw footage from war zones, invaded territories, crime scenes, disaster zones, and . . . the Knockout Game. Ultimately, regardless of our individual viewing preferences and disinclinations, real violence and brutality are inescapable components of contemporary media violence.

How do audiences respond to these videos? What kinds of emotions do we experience when we witness real violence? Can we distinguish between staged violence featuring professional stunts-persons and real physical assaults? Are there differences in how we cognitively interpret these two very different categories of media violence? And finally, what about our emotional responses toward victims of real violence? Does the plethora of graphic violence that saturates current entertainment media increasingly numb our senses? Or do we still retain the ability to empathize with these unfortunate victims of violence?

These questions constitute the crux of this research project. My goal is to examine how viewers cognitively and emotionally engage with the victims of real media violence in Knockout Game videos. Media effects research encompasses a well-established tradition of exploring audience responses to fictional media narratives and characters. But very little research has focused on this emerging media genre, and we consequently know very little about precisely how viewers construe *real* media violence. Therefore, before we can begin investigating these perplexing cognitive and affective responses, it may prove useful to first review existing scholarship in the arena of cognitive and emotional reactions to media characters.

TWO

Emotional Responses to Media Characters

You probably have a favorite TV show (or, if you are like me, several shows). And you probably also experience strong emotional feelings toward certain characters on these shows. Maybe you felt a surge of joy when Jim finally proposed to Pam on *The Office*, or a pang of sadness when *Glee*'s Sue Sylvester discovered that her baby had Down's syndrome. You find yourself rooting for the amateur gymnast who struggles to balance on two wine bottles on *America's Got Talent*. Perhaps, you are inexplicably drawn to the deliciously manipulative Frank Underwood on *House of Cards*, and inadvertently catch your breath when a wily reporter threatens to expose his scheming. Your own pulse races as *24*'s Jack Bauer races against the clock to thwart fanatical terrorists. This is also true for favorite movies, wherein we develop emotional bonds with certain characters who win either our sympathy or animosity as the storyline develops.

Emotions are powerful motivators and are also an integral aspect of the entertainment viewing experience. The feelings that we experience enable us to enjoy some genres and formats more than others. As viewers, we feel a range of emotions toward the media characters that we encounter. This is perhaps most evident in young children, who visibly display strong sentiments toward liked characters. Writers, directors, and cinematographers often provide explicit cues through plot elements, character development (particularly in the case of television series), and visual composition that prompt and facilitate specific emotional responses. But where do our feelings come from? Are they purely affective feeling states? Or do emotions also entail a corresponding rational element? Are the emotions that we feel toward media characters different from those that we experience in real life? These questions are addressed in the upcoming chapter. However, before we examine media characters, it may be useful to determine what exactly constitutes an emotion in the first place.

WHAT ARE EMOTIONS?

An emotion is a specific physiological, phenomenological, and expressive bodily response that directs an individual's attention toward a particular environment stimulus. Theorists have determined that this response also involves some degree of cognition about the given stimulus (Levinson 1997). The exact mechanics underlying the extent and interaction of the cognitive (thinking) versus affective (feeling) components continues to be a topic of theoretical debate. While some experts consider the cognitive component, that is, the belief or thought about that stimulus, to be the primary motivator (Bandura 2001; Zillmann 1991), others argue that the affective aspect is much more significant—particularly with regard to the emotional responses that we experience toward fictional stimuli (Gerrig 1993). This conclusion thus seems to infer that fiction has the potential to generate more intense emotions than nonfiction. As tempting and convenient as this conclusion may be, I am convinced that most of us can doubtless recollect real-life experiences that prompted very strong emotional responses indeed. Overall, most scholars agree that the cognitive and affective facets of our emotions are complementary and inter-related (Carroll 1997; Konijn and Hoorn 2005; Levinson 1997; Vorderer, Klimmt, and Ritterfeld 2004). A simple example may help illustrate how these components function in tandem.

If you were to encounter a dog as you walk down the street, your emotional response to the animal will depend on two interlinked processes. The cognitive aspect is the mental processing of the environmental stimulus itself, in this case something along the lines of, "I see a dog." The affective aspect, however, concerns your subjective predisposition toward dogs in general. Perhaps you are very fond of dogs and have a pet dog at home. If this is so, you are likely to experience positive affect toward the stimulus, and you may smile and stoop to scratch its head. On the other hand, if you do not like dogs and have had the misfortune of a bad canine-related past experience, you will quite possibly experience negative affect toward the animal and look to create maximum distance between the dog and yourself. The combination of these two aspects thus determines your emotional response to the stimulus as you either cheerily approach the dog or hastily withdraw from it. However, both components must exist in order for you to experience an emotion. Therefore, our emotional responses toward people, things, or events are contingent on some degree of comprehension and cognitive processing, as well as a corresponding affective disposition. Furthermore, emotional responses tend to be dynamic and evolve in response to changing situational cues. Let us revisit the first scenario, and assume that your friendly advance toward the dog is met with a snarl and angry snap. This negative experience is now likely to impact your future affective inclinations and subsequent emotional responses toward canines (and this particular animal, no doubt!).

This same dynamic applies to emotions generated by media content, as we simultaneously process (cognitive) and experience feelings (affective element) toward the entertainment media that we consume. However, although the affective ingredient may be relatively easy for most of us to locate and identify, the cognitive attribute is significantly more intricate and complex. Therefore, in order to understand our emotional responses to media content, it is important to understand exactly how we cognitively process real versus fictional stimuli.

COGNITIVE PROCESSING AND EVALUATING REALISM

Sustained and concentrated cognitive effort is hard work. Although we may prefer to think of ourselves as deliberate rational beings who devote our entire mental capacity to carefully evaluate each and every environmental stimulus, the truth is that we do not. Indeed, we *cannot*, because this would require an incredible expenditure of cognitive energy and mental effort. Occasionally, some circumstances and events may require careful mental scrutiny and processing. However, most day-to-day cognitive processing—especially media consumption—actually entails a far more economical process.

Simply put, we are cognitive misers who prefer to expend minimal mental effort to effectively process incoming stimuli, including media content. We accomplish this by way of developing and using schemata, or mental shortcuts (Raney 2003). A schema is a cognitive network that facilitates quick identification and comprehension of external cues. Familiar patterns and their comprising units constitute these networks. For example, consider one particular staple of horror movies and multiple key elements that enable us to identify and process it: a dilapidated and possibly damaged structure, abandoned and empty with no signs of recent occupation, ill-tended grounds and overgrown vegetation, no vehicles or means of transportation nearby, a forbidding thick forest all around, and (of course, the inevitable) rusty disused tools and other sharp implements in the immediate vicinity. At this point, we have enough details to recognize and retrieve the relevant schema: the lonely abandoned cabin in the woods. Regardless of any additional features that are later thrown into the mix, the schema ensures that we now have enough information to proceed. The presence of certain key details therefore determines which particular schemata get triggered.

Once activated, these cognitive networks then guide expectations with respect to what should or should not happen. As a result of the frequent activation of specific schemata—based on genre preferences, for instance—some cognitive networks necessarily have higher accessibility than others. For example, a horror movie fan may accurately predict that the tired and lost travelers will inevitably go against their better judgment and decide to spend the night at the lonely cabin in the woods. Additionally, a horror movie aficionado may also anticipate several gory encounters between these ill-fated travelers and the aforementioned sharp rusty implements before the night is through. Schemata therefore help us to efficiently navigate and organize countless crowding details of incoming stimuli.

Some scholars claim that the schemata reserved for fictional media are different from those that are used to process real-life events, because the former impose a narrative structure along with corresponding expectations on incoming fictional information (Busselle and Bilandzic 2008). However, problems can arise when story schemata become increasingly applied to non-story situations simply as a result of high accessibility and frequent activation. In such situations, the cognitive frameworks that are typically reserved to interpret and evaluate fictional characters can get applied to real-world people and situations. For example, an avid viewer of *CSI* and *NCIS* may apply the schema that helps her identify suspects on the show to observing her neighbor's behavior, becoming convinced that his irregular work hours, night-time visitors, and several tattoos and piercings necessarily imply that he is trafficking illegal narcotics from his residence. We occasionally encounter disturbing news reports that attest to the misguided tragic outcomes of transferring fictional schemata to real life. The recent brutal attack perpetrated by two eighth-grade girls who lured their friend into the woods and stabbed her multiple times in order to ingratiate themselves to a fictitious character dubbed Slender Man (Walsh, October 22, 2014) is one such instance. It is therefore not unreasonable to assume that some viewers who enjoy violent media content on a regular basis may begin to apply these fictional schemata to process real-world violence. For these desensitized individuals, real-world attacks and assaults are essentially interpreted and construed as though they were fictional events. This in turn has sobering implications for how we emotionally respond to the victims of real violence.

How does information get mentally tagged as real or fictional in the first place? How do we decide what is real or not? The schemata that we use to sort incoming content are but one half of the picture. The next step involves the actual assimilation and comprehension of sorted information. At this point, the mind decides whether to accept it as real (and therefore true) or reject it as false (fictional and therefore not genuine). Two competing perspectives attempt to explain how comprehension occurs in the human mind (Gilbert, Krull, and Malone 1990). The first of these is known as the Cartesian model, according to which understanding and believing are separate and sequential psychological functions. This means that incoming information must first be understood, following which its veracity is determined. On the basis of this assessment, the information may then either be accepted or rejected. Let us consider a couple of examples of Cartesian thinking. Assume that a reputable news source informs its viewers of a local salmonella outbreak. Cartesian processing involves comprehending the message content, and then determining its veracity. Once the message has been understood, it is now necessary to gauge its authenticity. Since the message was received from a reputable news organization, let us assume that you are confident that this source checks and verifies its facts prior to broadcasting the information. You may thus conclude that the information is true and believe that a salmonella outbreak has indeed occurred. Now consider that you are watching a popular fiction fantasy media text, such as *Game of Thrones* or *The Hobbit*. An armor-clad warrior atop the castle battlements leaps off the edge, only to be swooped up from below by a magnificent glittering dragon. According to the Cartesian model, your mind would first comprehend this information, namely, that the warrior has leapt to his apparent doom and has been rescued by a powerful dragon. The next step involves determining the veracity of this information. This is trickier. Warriors adorned in armor do (or did, more accurately) exist historically, as do castles. However, dragons are creatures of myth and fantasy and do not really exist. Your mind thus rejects this information as false (not reality) and does not believe that it actually occurred, even though you still comprehend it. Therefore, although the dragon might exist within the confines of the narrative and media text, this creature—and by extension, the text—get mentally tagged as fictional and not real.

However, research in this area shows strong support for the second theoretical perspective, known as the Spinozan model (Gilbert et al. 1990). This theory advocates a very different perspective: "all ideas are accepted (i.e., represented in the mind as true) *prior* to a rational analysis of their veracity, and some ideas are subsequently *unaccepted* (i.e., rerepresented as false)" (Gilbert et al. 1990, 601). In other words, according to the Spinozan model, comprehension and belief are simultaneous processes. Returning to our earlier examples, this means that you would perceive and accept both the salmonella outbreak news report and the scene with the dragon as equally real and true at the time of processing. In retrospect, you could choose to revisit the dragon scene (perhaps after the movie has ended) and remind yourself that it was fiction because dragons do not really exist. However, this process of retrospective rejection requires additional cognitive effort after the fact and thus may not appeal to all individuals across the board. In this sense, the Spinozan approach complements schema theory because both perspectives advocate cognitive economy. To summarize, regardless of whether viewers are exposed to real or fictional information, the Spinozan model of comprehension and perceived realism suggests that any information is accepted as real and true *regardless* of its fictionality.

This means that our default processing mode is to not evaluate the realism of a narrative, unless we are prompted by some cue within the program (for example, narrative inconsistency), or by an external source (Busselle, Ryabovolova, and Wilson 2004). For instance, we are unlikely to question the realism of a media text unless its special effects are particularly hokey and awkward, or if a character who is supposedly fatally injured still manages to fend off a horde of villains. Or a particularly irritating friend enjoys interrupting movie screenings by gleefully pointing out anachronistic script and production elements, such as observing that cellphones did not exist in the 1940s. Similarly, apparent production and post-production techniques such as camera angles, scripting, and character positioning allow most of us to differentiate between so-called "reality" television shows and raw footage of real events. Some genres and their accompanying schemata allow for a more flexible construction of realism, as in the case of science fiction and fantasy which require some level of suspended belief on the part of the audience to ensure enjoyment. Researchers have identified several conceptual variables that influence the perceived realism of media narratives, including probability (the likelihood that something observed on television actually exists in the real world), plausibility (events or behaviors that could potentially occur in the real world), and social realism or factuality (how accurately a depicted event or person represents a real world person or event) (Busselle et al. 2004; Hall 2003).

Yet ultimately, a sentimental historical drama, slapstick comedy, or action extravaganza will all be accepted and processed by viewers as genuine and real at the time of viewing. On reflection, some particularly vigilant and better-informed viewers may disregard these as fictional. Over time, most of us learn to look for indicators of a media narrative's factual realism, although this propensity for cognitive effort varies from one person to another. Allow me to illustrate by way of a personal experience. As someone who professes an amateur interest in Italian Renaissance history, I was extremely impressed by Showtime's *The Borgias*. The gorgeous and historically accurate costumes, superb cinematography, fascinating attention to production and set design details, and brilliant script had me convinced that this was a faithful depiction of one of history's most notorious families. Propelled by the compelling narrative to learn more about the Borgias, I sadly discovered that the glittering production was actually rife with historical inaccuracies. In retrospect, a lot of the details that I had accepted as true did not really occur and needed to therefore be tagged as creative license (fiction). Yet, for other viewers who did not follow up with additional reading on the historical Borgias, the series constitutes actual fact. Realism evaluation is therefore an acquired and learned trait and is conspicuously absent among very young viewers, who are inclined to believe that their favorite cartoon characters really exist.

So far, we have determined that emotional responses consist of an affective feeling component and a rational cognitive component. This cognitive aspect is further influenced by which particular schemata are activated to organize incoming information, as well as by the Spinozan tendency to unquestioningly accept all incoming information as true. But this process prompts some interesting questions about emotional responses to unpleasant or dysphoric media content. In other words, when confronted with disturbing and graphic images of violence and tragedy, do we necessarily and implicitly accept it all as true? If that were the case, the valence of corresponding emotional responses should be consistent with the unpleasant content. Watching an innocent character get assaulted by criminals should thus prompt feelings of fear and sadness among viewers. Yet we often find that audiences demonstrate varied responses to unpleasant media content, whether these be images of war and crime, or random Knockout Game videos of brutal assaults on unsuspecting victims. Indeed, a quick glance through comments posted below these videos indicates that although some viewers do express shock and outrage at Knockout Game attacks, several other individuals actually consider these filmed assaults to be amusing and entertaining. What accounts for these vastly different emotional responses? The key to this puzzle may be found in understanding how empathy and affective dispositions to media characters influence media enjoyment.

AFFECTIVE DISPOSITIONS TOWARD MEDIA CHARACTERS

The origin of the term "empathy" is traditionally traced back to the use of the German word *Einfühlung* in the early twentieth century which literally translates as "feeling oneself into something" (Feagin 1997; Zillmann 1994; 2006). This definition has evolved over time to express the degree to which an individual notices and is concerned about another being's needs and concerns (Detert, Trevino, and Sweitzer 2008). With regard to media and fictional content, empathy can be thought of as sharing the feelings of a character (Cohen 2001; Vorderer et al. 2004). This project subscribes to Zillmann's (1991) definition of empathy as "a feeling state that is thought to be brought on by the observation of a fellow being in a specific situation" (140). Furthermore, empathy requires that this feeling must be hedonically compatible and concordant with the observed experience. This means that an empathic response to another person's sadness would be to experience a corresponding dip in your own spirits, as you experience sympathy or pity for their misfortune. By contrast, experiencing amusement or mirth at someone else's misery would not constitute an empathic response. Empathy is important because it plays an integral role in how we emotionally respond to media characters within the narrative context.

According to affective disposition theory (ADT) (Zillmann and Cantor 1976) we experience media enjoyment as a result of our affective dispositions (or inclinations) toward characters and their narrative outcomes. Our enjoyment increases when something good happens to a character that we like, or when unpleasant things happen to disliked characters (Raney 2003). Consider an inspirational college sport drama, such as *We Are Marshall* or *Hoosiers*. Over the course of the movie, the protagonists gain our growing empathy and emotional support as we watch them strive to develop athletic prowess while overcoming incredible odds. We watch the emergence of a budding team spirit, dedication, loyalty, and respect for their new coach. We are practically willing them to succeed in that all-important final confrontation against their rivals. Our own spirits surge as the winning point is scored and we watch our heroes prevail. And we cannot deny the stab of satisfaction that we feel as the bitter scheming of an arrogant rival coach, obnoxious opposing athlete, or discouraging local authority is thwarted by this glorious victory. Our propensity to empathize with them makes media characters more real to us, more believable.

A number of additional textual factors can promote or discourage empathy, evoking greater identification with some characters than others. For instance, first-person narratives invite a more personal relationship with the story-teller compared to a detached third-person perspective (Oatley 1999). Editing and visual composition can also impact empathy. The closer we are to the action and a character's emotions, the more connected we feel to their plight.

These affective dispositions toward characters are preceded by our moral evaluations of their actions and motivations within the narrative (Raney 2003). In other words, we are more likely to approve of (and therefore support) a protagonist who is driven by noble motives and goals. This positive moral evaluation of her actions then facilitates a corresponding positive disposition toward this character. Similarly, characters who resort to dishonorable tactics and aspire to unworthy ambitions seldom gain our approval. Instead, this moral disapproval of their goals and actions is more likely to evoke negative dispositions. For example, let us consider a gritty serial killer drama, such as *The Silence of the Lambs* or *Se7en*. According to ADT, the young detective who endeavors to uncover the serial killer and save future victims gains a positive moral evaluation from us viewers because she is motivated to act for the greater good, setting aside personal safety to protect the innocent and vulnerable. We thus develop a positive disposition toward the detective, which then allows us to empathize with her predicament. This in turn encourages us to experience greater enjoyment when she succeeds, or concern when her safety is threatened. On the other hand, the vicious killer who is primarily driven by personal ambition and a sadistic need to inflict suffering receives a resoundingly negative moral evaluation. We do not approve of his actions and therefore develop a negative disposition toward him, hoping that he will ultimately be thwarted. And we are happy when the law finally catches up with him and the killer receives a fitting punishment for his crimes.

One of ADT's pitfalls is the implication that moral evaluations of characters' motives and actions are contingent on the viewer's continual appraisal of every character's action throughout the narrative. Think about it. This means that in order to decide how much we like or dislike the detective, her boss, her boss's assistant, the other detectives on the force, the killer, the killer's victims, the victims' families and so forth, we would have to be consistently monitoring each and every one of these characters over the course of the media narrative. This is a substantial expenditure of cognitive energy, especially in the case of television series that span several episodes. This process would doubtless leave us mentally and emotionally exhausted! Most of us watch movies and TV for a respite from otherwise demanding jobs and daily commitments. So it is reasonable to assume that we seek more mental shortcuts so as to expend minimal cognitive effort and yet still enjoy the media content. One useful strategy is to rely on schemata or character models (Busselle and Bilandzic 2008) when forming initial dispositions toward characters. This means that we look for certain clues or key details in those crucial early establishing scenes of a narrative that provide information about a given character's moral and ethical inclinations. This lets us know whether the character is one of the "good guys" or "bad guys." We can then establish a corresponding affective disposition toward the character. For example, most action/disaster movies typically begin with a cozy domestic scene where we see the protagonist at home with loved ones. Little details like waking up the kids, eating breakfast with the family, and sending them off to school help us speedily access and draw on the "loving parent" character model—itself a mental shortcut to informing us that this is one of the "good guys." By contrast, the villain is typically established early in the narrative as a cold, ruthless, and ambitious person who will stop at nothing to get what he wants. These details at the outset of the narrative typically hint at who we are expected to like and support, whose side we are encouraged to take. It is important to note that such strategies are not automatically successful at manipulating viewers' emotions. In some cases, audiences may display indifference to the characters, as indicated by a lack of emotional reaction and attachment (Raney 2003; 2006). And in other circumstances, such attempts may backfire completely, leading to counterempathy or negative dispositions toward protagonists (Zillmann 1994; Zillmann and Knobloch 2001). Such instances are not the norm, however, and contemporary television shows increasingly display more sophisticated scripts and character development. Of particular interest is the growing popularity and appeal of morally ambiguous heroes (Oliver and Krakowiak 2009)—flawed protagonists who are neither entirely good nor bad—such as Don Draper on *Mad Men*, Dexter on the hit Showtime series of the same name, Frank Underwood on *House of Cards*, and *Breaking Bad's* Walter White, to name a few. These villains with a heart of gold have mixed motives and their actions are seldom entirely commendable. Yet for some reason, they are compelling characters that inexplicably draw us to care about them.

For the most part, ADT remains a useful framework to examine emotional relationships with media characters. Affective and cognitive responses have been shown to predict moral judgments of plot characters (Raney and Bryant 2002), that then play a crucial role in determining the extent to which we empathize with these characters (Zillmann 1994; Raney et al. 2009). A particular variant of empathy is of particular interest to this project.

Empathic distress refers to a specific subcategory of empathy, and is best described as a hedonically negative affective response that is provoked by "witnessing a liked protagonist suffer from . . . distressing conditions and events" (de Wied, Zillmann, and Ordman 1994). To clarify, empathic distress is an emotional reaction that we are likely to experience from watching another person's misfortune. It is frequently characterized by feelings of anxiety, sadness, and/or tension. This concern also increases if we like, or have a positive affiliation for, the person in distress (Hoffner and Cantor 1991). In the area of media research, empathic distress is particularly useful for investigating how viewers feel toward characters whose welfare is threatened or who are injured in the course of the narrative, such as victims of violence. It therefore makes sense that the more we like a particular character, the more empathic distress we are likely to experience when this character is in physical, emotional, or psychological danger. Powerful dramatic portrayals can prompt considerable empathic distress among audiences. Think back to movies that profoundly moved you. Perhaps you can remember how you felt when you first watched *Schindler's List*, or HBO's *Band of Brothers*, or even Disney's *Bambi* or *The Lion King*. Strangely enough, empathic distress is strongly linked to greater media enjoyment, particularly in the case of narratives that have happy endings. Although this may seem counterintuitive at first, it is easily explained by way of the relief that a viewer experiences when a liked protagonist successfully rallies against the odds to emerge unscathed at the end of the narrative. As ADT outlines, enjoyment results from seeing liked characters succeed, and this enjoyment is enhanced when a character overcomes significant difficulties along the way.

In an interesting experiment, de Wied and her colleagues (1994) investigated the role of empathic distress in dramatic tearjerkers and overall enjoyment at the movies. Participants watched the classic 1989 movie *Steel Magnolias*, which focuses on the personal ups and downs of a group of close-knit female friends. The researchers paused the film at three particularly poignant moments so that participants could record their current emotional reactions. At the end of the film, viewers also completed overall enjoyment and trait empathy surveys. Analysis of the data revealed that although high trait empathizers recorded stronger emotional reactions during the movie than low trait empathizers, they subsequently enjoyed the film more. In a similar experiment, Raney and Bryant (2002) demonstrated that high trait empathizers were more likely to sympathize with the victim of a dramatic media crime. These same individuals were also more likely to enjoy narratives in which the crime against this victim was avenged. Vorderer and his colleagues (2004) note that empathy is a function of two attributes: the ability to empathize, and one's readiness to do so. Some of us are inherently more predisposed to empathize than others (Detert et al. 2008), and greater empathic distress prefaces greater enjoyment when the narrative reaches a satisfying conclusion. So this suggests that although trait empathy levels may vary from one individual to the next, with some of us being more likely to empathize and at greater levels than others, high empathizers typically experience greater enjoyment at the end of an emotionally tumultuous narrative.

At this point, it is important to note that human responses to media content are frequently dynamic and unpredictable across time, and most disposition-based theories of media enjoyment recognize this fact. We do not always react in exactly the same way with exactly the same emotional responses to similar media content. To a large extent, your emotional responses at any given time are influenced by several trait-level variables, including the mood that you are in at that moment, your ability and willingness to concentrate on the narrative, and your attitude toward a specific genre (Raney 2006). Consider the difference between trying to watch a long-awaited sequel to your favorite movie franchise at a noisy theater, consistently interrupted by other viewers' conversations and blinking cellphones, and watching this same movie undisturbed in the comfort of your home. Which of these two experiences are you more likely to enjoy? Similarly, complex storylines and character developments, as in movies such as *Eternal Sunshine of the Spotless Mind* and *Inception,* are difficult to follow when you are simultaneously multi-tasking in the kitchen or trying to finish a report. Distracted viewing interferes with the extent to which viewers form affective dispositions toward media characters.

So we now know that we rely on character models and schemata to help us identify heroes and villains in a narrative. We also use similar cognitive shortcuts to decide whether or not a character's motives and actions and morally acceptable. These moral judgments then allow us to like some characters and dislike others. Empathic distress is a negative emotional response that we feel when we experience concern for a liked character. When narratives end in a satisfactory manner that delivers anticipated outcomes to liked and disliked characters, we experience enjoyment of that specific media content. This is a good start.

But it still does not explain how audiences manage the uncomfortable and negative feelings prompted by unresolved media narratives that contain disturbing and distressing images. For instance, in Knockout Game and "happy slapping" videos, there is seldom a traditional media narrative and never a happy conclusion. Instead the viewer encounters a vicious and violent scene that abruptly ends with no resolution for attacker or victim. So how do viewers manage empathic distress in these situations? And what could possibly account for those who claim to enjoy this kind of content? The next chapter explains how empathic distress can be minimized by morally reconstruing dysphoric media content.

THREE

Moral Disengagement and Enjoying Media Violence

Humans are inventive and resourceful creatures and we can often find creative ways to rationalize and reconstrue situations to our advantage through some clever self-talk. As social agents, we have the ability to choose and act in any context (Bandura 1999). This also implies that we have the inherent power to behave in a moral and compassionate manner, or to exercise reprehensible and inhumane actions. According to noted psychologist Albert Bandura (1999), we are self-regulating and self-reflexive beings, with the ability to assess the moral imperative of our actions before we commit them. In other words, we possess an in-built sense of what is right and wrong, and thus have the power to regulate and manage our behavior in accordance with this set of values. Despite this, however, we sometimes do things that we know to be wrong. Why and how does this happen?

In this chapter, we shall explore the fascinating realm of moral disengagement. First, I review some common disengagement strategies, and then proceed to how these and other cognitive coping strategies pertain to media enjoyment.

MORAL DISENGAGEMENT STRATEGIES

Over time, we are inculcated into a structure that bestows particular external values and social sanctions (Bandura 1999). Young children soon learn appropriate and acceptable behaviors, and also learn that unacceptable behaviors will be met with negative consequences. This process continues throughout one's life, as different environments and contexts teach us their corresponding rules and regulations for acceptable behavior. In addition to these, there are certain inherent fundamental values that most of us would instantly agree to, for example, that stealing and murder are wrong. These values are an integral part of our inner moral selves, and we rely on them to regulate our own behavior. As Bandura notes, "in this self-regulatory process, people monitor their conduct and the condition under which it occurs, judge it in relation to their moral standards and perceived circumstances, and regulate their actions by the consequences they apply to themselves" (193). We thus learn to automatically monitor our environments and adapt our behavior accordingly. For example, at a local fruit-seller's stall, the pears look exceptionally tasty and succulent. I could easily sneak a pear into my pocket and wander off without her knowledge. Yet my inner moral sense—some might refer to this as my conscience—tells me that this would be wrong. So I choose to regulate my actions in accordance with my internal moral standards.

However, Bandura says that we can decide when to apply these internal moral self-sanctions, that is, when to listen to our conscience. Disregarding moral self-sanctions allows us to act in inhumane and reprehensible ways, and do things that we know to be wrong. This process is labeled moral disengagement—that is, deliberately and intentionally disengaging moral self-sanctions to engage in immoral acts—and can only occur when we *choose* to deactivate moral monitoring mechanisms. As social agents, we have the ability to decide when we want to trigger and utilize these regulatory processes, and when to ignore them. Bandura outlines eight moral disengagement strategies that allow us to rationalize lapses in moral judgment. Depending on how successfully we deploy them, we can emerge relatively unscathed and exonerate ourselves of any culpability or wrongdoing.

Moral Justification

This strategy reconstrues the purpose of a reprehensible act, positioning it as necessary in order to achieve a noble or worthy cause. In this way, immoral actions can be excused and overlooked because they ultimately endorse a far more important and honorable prerogative. This strategy is probably applicable to most media violence portrayals, because the hero must batter villains and destroy opponents to secure an important goal—such as rescuing vulnerable loved ones, saving cities from imminent destruction, or protecting some scarce and valuable resource. Recasting his crimes as valorous yet necessary evils allows us to overlook the inherent wrongdoing, and still view the hero in a favorable light. Such thinking has spawned crusades and other violent fanatical endeavors, as individuals convince themselves that violence is imperative for glory and the greater good. Suicide bombers and other terrorist actors also reflect this warped thinking, and firmly believe that a greater noble reward justifies violence against innocent people.

Euphemistic Labeling

Sometimes referred to as verbal sanitization, euphemistic labeling functions discursively to replace offensive and controversial vocabulary with comparatively innocuous and ambiguous terminology. Consider, for example, those who refer to innocent civilian casualties of war as "collateral damage," or reports that avoid details of the dead and wounded by merely stating that "The uprising has been *neutralized.*" The latter terms are completely devoid of humane connotations. It is therefore far easier to commit atrocities when they don't *sound* like atrocities. Euphemistic labeling also occurs in more mundane contexts, such as when I pocket office supplies by claiming that I am "merely borrowing" them. On some level, euphemistic labeling goes well beyond simply sugarcoating the truth, because it involves a deliberate and manipulative attempt to deflect public attention from reprehensible actions by giving them less sinister labels. "The Knockout Game" and "happy slapping" are perfect examples, because these titles discursively recast brutal random attacks as little more than trivial fun and amusement, similar to children's playground games. Euphemistic labeling whitewashes ugly truths, disguising things that we know to be wrong as palatable and harmless.

Advantageous Comparison

In the earlier example, had I attempted to steal a pear from the fruit-vendor, and my less-than-dexterous attempt drawn the vendor's attention and anger, I could respond to her accusations with, "Relax, will you? It was just one pear. I am not grabbing your entire stock!" This strategy, known as advantageous comparison, reconstrues immoral acts to make them seem less severe by comparing them to far worse outcomes. The teenager who returns her mother's car with a broken tail light and retorts, "It's not like I wrecked the car!" is also utilizing advantageous comparison. Things just do not seem that bad when they are compared against horrendous alternatives. Of course, this does not excuse the original wrongdoing in the first place. Advantageous comparison therefore attempts to distract from an offense by contrasting it with something much worse, in a manner that diminishes the original offense.

Displacement of Responsibility

Sometimes, terrible actions are committed by social agents who later claim that they were not acting of their own free will, but merely following the orders of a higher authority. Remember the Nuremberg trials? Or consider the torture allegations against prison guards at Guantanamo and Abu Ghraib. In these instances, responsibility for committing a reprehensible act is shifted to another target, and the original actor thus tries to absolve himself of any crime. After all, he is just a vessel for implementing someone else's orders. This line of thinking minimizes the proactive agentic perspective that we are responsible for our own actions because they stem from individual choices. In other words, regardless of the inherent wrongness of my actions, at the end of the day I still retain the ability to decide whether or not to commit them. Horrific crimes are often carried out by entirely reasonable and decent people simply because they blindly and unquestioningly follow the directives of authority figures, as in the case of the infamous Milgram shock experiments.

Diffusion of Responsibility

This particular strategy derives from mob mentality and the power of collective action. In these situations, immoral acts are deemed permissible because they are simultaneously committed by several people at the same time. Responsibility for the wrongdoing thus cannot be attributed to any one person, and is diffused and distributed among many agents. This enables ordinary people to get swept up in the passion of the moment and safety of large numbers, and engage in behavior that they would otherwise oppose. Consider the damage and violence committed by rioters and irate protestors. Or even the brutalities committed by law enforcement authorities and military personnel simply because "everyone else was doing it." In some ways, this sinister form of peer pressure occurs mainly because of the flawed perception that if several people are simultaneously doing something wrong, no one person is individually responsible for the action. The simple truth, however, is that we are all accountable for our actions and their outcomes all the time. Diffusion of responsibility provides the illusion of security because it becomes more difficult to pin blame on a single actor. Many forms of bullying, and cyberbullying in particular, stem from the diffusion of responsibility. The Stanford Prison Experiment serves as a disturbing reminder of the dangers of collective action through immoral group decision-making. It is easy to perpetrate crimes against others when there is little impetus to remain personally accountable for your actions.

Minimizing or Ignoring the Consequences

In some cases, the outcome of wrongdoing and harm can be overlooked or distorted to minimize the apparent injury. How convenient it is for a drone operator to navigate the weapon from across oceans and never have to personally confront the significant damage and loss of lives. Comfortably insulated in our middle-class lives, it is easy to ignore or disregard the harm and suffering wreaked by our tax dollars in distant lands. The employee who systematically siphons off cash from executive accounts can do so thinking that he is embezzling from a nameless and faceless corporation, instead of real people. Most often associated with convoluted hierarchies that isolate perpetrators from the outcomes of their actions, this disengagement strategy is also surprisingly applicable to media violence. As Barbara Osborn observed, TV violence does not bleed. We rarely witness the results and effects of violence on its victims. Media narratives typically privilege the hero's perspective, and our affective dispositions encourage us to share and defend this perspective. Yes, Jack Bauer had to "rough up" that terrorist a bit to find out where the bomb was planted. But he was doing it for the greater good, and besides the villain didn't seem too injured, right? Mainly surface and flesh wounds. Those should heal up just fine. Sure enough, when the villain bounces back relatively unharmed two episodes later, our previous nonchalance is reinforced and we learn to worry less about villains. Gorgeous and awe-inspiring special effects also play a role in sweeping us up in sheer grandeur, and we care little for the sheer havoc inflicted on inhabitants of a building that gets caught in the crossfire, bursting into flames as the Avengers pursue alien forces of evil emanating from an intergalactic vortex. Desensitization to violence thrives on a lack of empathy, and this strategy is well suited to cultivating indifference among media audiences.

Dehumanization

The last two disengagement strategies entail distorting one's perception of the victim of a reprehensible act. Dehumanization casts the victim as inferior and sub-human, and thus not worthy of our empathy or concern. This strategy works particularly well with unknown and strange others, people who hail from different cultural and ethnic backgrounds. It is easy to demonize strangers with whom we have little in common and thus cast them as threatening or intimidating. This strategy was successfully employed by the Third Reich to dehumanize and target Jews, gypsies, homosexuals, and other reviled groups. It was also successfully deployed during the Kosovo crisis to aid the ethnic genocide on both sides of the war. The us-them dynamic takes on a particularly sinister twist when outsiders are perceived as barbarians, infidels, monsters, and villains. It is not surprising that most media antagonists and villains are dehumanized so that we do not feel terribly upset when bad things happen to them. Media villains are often the targets of exaggerated dehumanization in an effort to ensure that they are unlikable and disagreeable, so that the audience seldom sympathizes with their goals and motives. Sadistic freaks with insatiable appetites for pain and suffering, cold and calculating megalomaniacs who plot mass destruction, blood-crazed fiends who will let nothing and no one stand in their way, faceless goons who owe blind allegiance to a tyrant—we have encountered them in our media narratives with relatively high frequency. Dehumanizing them makes our hero seem all the more noble, worthy, and human-like. ADT postulates that we also experience enjoyment when bad events befall disliked characters. It's so much easier to empathize with the protagonist and support his goals, even if he does occasionally have to get his hands dirty dispatching one or more of these villains. Video games are a particularly appropriate example of this, as players battle aliens, monsters, and other supernatural horrors that bear little resemblance to human beings.

Attributive Blame

Finally, this last disengagement strategy flips the tables on the victim. Attributive blame places blame for the immoral act solely on the victim by saying that he/she did something to deserve it. In doing so, the perpetrator is absolved of blame, and the victim becomes responsible for their misfortune. This strategy explains rape myths that blame a victim for being in a particular place, engaging in particular actions, or wearing a specific outfit. She knew that alleyway was unsafe, so why did she choose to enter it? What did she expect, wearing that short skirt and those high heels? In some cases, it is also easier to blame the circumstances for one's behavior rather than take full responsibility for one's wrongdoing. For instance, it was acceptable to taze the suspect because he seemed to be reaching for a weapon in a crowded area. Or he should not have left his credit card lying around unless he intended for me to use it. Attributive blame transfers responsibility for the wrongdoing in such a manner that the perpetrator convinces herself that *she* is the victim in this situation. This creative rationalizing is also employed by bullies who justify attacking victims who "look like dorks" or "had it coming." This blame thus situates an attack as both inevitable and warranted.

Bandura (1999) describes these moral disengagement strategies as ways to justify and explain away immoral behavior. But I argue that, as media consumers, we use many of these same strategies to enhance media enjoyment. And this is especially true for audiences who enjoy dysphoric media genres, such as horror and violence.

DISENGAGEMENT AND COGNITIVE COPING STRATEGIES

How do you conceptualize exceptionally distressing or unpleasant media content? Perhaps you define this as a creepy and chilling atmospheric horror, like the recent *American Horror Story* series. Or perhaps it is an action extravaganza replete with brutal choreographed fight sequences, splintering bones, and gushing arteries, such as in the graphic-novel inspired features *Sin City* and *Watchmen*. In my case, this would be elaborate historical portrayals of torture and abuse, as in the case of a recent drama that featured a particularly intricate and realistic portrayal of a slave lynching. We live in an era that is especially unsympathetic to sensitive souls who have no stomach for raw and profuse violence. As directors and producers compete for box office profits and audiences in an increasingly fragmented mediascape, movies and television shows alike strive to outdo each other in offering ever more explicit content.

Regardless of our individual thresholds for graphic and disturbing content, we all rely on some form of disengagement in order to endure (dare I say, sometimes enjoy) unpleasant media content. This involves utilizing a variety of tactics to diminish or prevent disturbing media content from truly upsetting us. In some cases, we may actually erect a physical barrier between ourselves and the screen. This is most evident in young children, who may cover their eyes with their hands or another object to avoid directly looking at something that frightens them. Perhaps you know adults who still peek from behind a cushion when they watch scary movies.

As adults, however, we tend to use the cognitive equivalent of this barrier to prevent disturbing media material from overwhelming us. Research indicates that we often employ rationalization processes to disregard unpleasant content that threatens overall media enjoyment. Audiences are generally aware of their physical separation from what they view on television or in a movie, and therefore "know that it never did happen . . . [or] never could happen" (Cantor 2002, 291). These coping strategies require the activation of cognitive processes to reduce or prevent the fear and discomfort induced by disturbing media content (Bryant and Thompson 2002). In other words, we do not completely engage with the viewing experience primarily because we know that we are watching a fictional representation with actors and professional stunt people (Zillmann 1994). This process is more applicable to some subgenres than others, for instance those that rely on explicit and gratuitous violence. If you have ever watched a Quentin Tarantino movie or the graphic-novel-to-screen adaptations of *300* and the afore-mentioned *Sin City*, you may be familiar with the sheer spectacle of spurting blood, bone-crunching combat, and mindless slaughter. Simultaneously, however, this special-effects extravaganza of ferocious brutality, although mesmerizing in its vivid portrayal of violence, is so far removed from reality that it is relatively easy to disregard the onscreen images—and any lingering dysphoria—in retrospect.

The same process becomes more challenging for less explicit violent subgenres, such as action movies and atmospheric horrors. When the violence appears to be more realistic, audiences must exert greater cognitive effort to remind themselves that these are actors performing a scripted narrative. Even though the violence seems plausible and comparatively generic, the motivated media consumer can remind herself that it is not real because it never really happened in the first place.

Viewers can thus enjoy the narrative while ultimately disregarding any gore and violence as merely the stuff of fiction.

It is significantly more difficult to discount violent portrayals in historical dramas. Realistic depictions of cruel tortures and executions in series such as *The Tudors, Vikings, Rome,* as well as portrayals of slavery in epics such as *Amistad* and *12 Years a Slave* contain historically accurate representations of real events. These events—or at least, events very much like them—did indeed occur to real people at some point in history. Yet, although mankind's capacity for cruelty and brutality may cause us to gasp and shudder in horror, it is still possible to insulate ourselves from experiencing genuine concern. A little voice in the back of our minds reminds us that the horrible images were ultimately *representations* and *enactments* of real events. In other words, the distress and shock that we experienced while watching these scenes are merely the result of gifted actors, creative makeup, and convincing special effects. Nobody actually got hurt during these disturbing sequences, and there are even disclaimers at the end of the credits to reassure us that the animals received humane treatment, too. Therefore, although we may still feel a twinge of discomfort and pity for the unfortunate historic characters themselves, we are so far removed from these people by time and space that the impact is significantly lessened. Those terrible things happened centuries ago, we tell ourselves, and surely people today do not resort to such barbarism and are much more civilized. Once again, therefore, cognitive rationalizing enables us to resolutely set aside discomforts and dysphoria, as we reassure ourselves that it was a realistic portrayal of bad things that happened a long time ago. Indeed, the increasing prevalence of behind-the-scenes featurettes that detail how exactly the special effects and makeup artists created such convincing representations of brutality supports and bolsters this category of coping mechanisms, while providing us with a more resilient arsenal of coping strategies for future utilization. Therefore, the vast majority of entertainment media genres allow us to cloak ourselves in the tenuous reassurance that the onscreen violence and injuries are fake. In turn, this coping mechanism allows us to actively avoid empathizing with the victims of violence because we tell ourselves that it did not really happen in the first place.

A byproduct of this cognitive coping technique is that we simultaneously disengage the moral self-sanctions that allow us to recognize the injurious outcomes of these violent acts (Bandura 2002). To clarify, knowing that the victims did not really suffer makes it easier to overlook the severity of the violence in the first place. Research has shown that individuals who frequently engage in reprehensible behavior use cognitive rationalization to justify their actions, and increasingly become less inhibited about acting in ways that conflict with their internal moral standards (Bandura, Barbaranelli, Caprara, and Pastorelli 1996; Bryant and Thompson 2002). The more we rely on these disengagement strategies to explain away bad conduct, the more accessible and available these rationalization processes become for future use. They are deployed so often that they practically become second nature, requiring significantly less cognitive work to locate and activate each time. It is not unreasonable to assume that extremely frequent usage may even make these coping strategies the default processing mode for heavy consumers of media violence. Specifically, attributive blame and minimizing the consequences may be particularly useful disengagement strategies to suggest that the victim deserved to be attacked, and also reject the onscreen violence as fictional, respectively. No matter how terrible the circumstances, most of us cannot deny feeling a surge of satisfaction when a villain receives his long-overdue punishment. Indeed, the more heinous an antagonist's crimes, the more outrageous the price that must subsequently be paid for them. It does not matter if the good guys resort to equally despicable tactics to overthrow the villains, because at the end of the day good must prevail. Several cues are present within fictional narrative structures that encourage us—particularly those among us who rely heavily on schematas—to disregard the nature and consequences of onscreen violence in these fictional narratives where the good guys eventually prevail. It is therefore entirely possible to watch a liked protagonist commit violent acts, all the while approving of his actions, because the moral disengagement process inhibits negative evaluations of the character's motivations and goals. The existing positive dispositions toward this hero are thus maintained, and the moral disengagement has fulfilled its purpose in enhancing media enjoyment. Media narratives typically consist of cleverly engineered scripts that often require viewers to trigger the attributive blame disengagement strategy in order to experience enjoyment. Additionally, most narratives will typically follow up these unpleasant scenes with happy ones of a hero's success and the return to a comfortable status quo. Likewise, minimizing the consequences of media violence ensures that we viewers pay little attention to the destructive and damaging aspects of violence, and instead glory in its sheer awe and magnificence. Most narratives culminate in a happy ending as the winners saunter off into the sunset (or some metaphorical equivalent), and we are denied information about the slow and painstaking reconstruction of damaged lives and property following the bloodbath. Considering that we are subjected to continual moral monitoring in our everyday lives, it is not really surprising that we morally disengage when given the chance to do so, even if it is only for the sake of media enjoyment (Raney 2003).

As viewers, we consistently make active decisions to disengage moral standards that would otherwise condemn displays of media violence. Not only does doing so enable us to enjoy the narrative. It also allows us to enjoy the violence itself. This is because a small percentage of the audience has actually had the opportunity to experience some of these situations firsthand. Among these might be those who have served in elite military corps, work in special weapons and crime task forces, and those who have been the victims of horrific crimes. Graphic media violence allows us to vicariously confront and "participate" in these terrifying situations, and therefore experience a fraction of the adrenaline rush, anxiety, and panic that the real context might provoke. Consider the spine-tingling scene toward the end of the movie *The Silence of the Lambs*, when Detective Clarice Starling is trapped in the serial killer's basement. Our pulses race as she attempts to hide from a man who clearly has the advantage of the dark environment. We feel what must be similar in some way (or at least we tell ourselves so) to the blind terror and sheer desperation of a trapped animal. Yet, unlike the animal or the character in the narrative, we can walk away from this horrible scenario whenever we choose to do so, or visually disconnect by looking away or shutting off the movie. We therefore experience these negative emotions and the accompanying thrill, but on our own terms. In other words, media violence allows us to safely indulge in the vicarious arousal of these disturbing stimuli "knowing full well that retreat from the situation is always open, and realizing that, after all, it is only a story" (Tannenbaum 1980, 121).

Most research on moral disengagement focuses on its impact on moral agency and aggressive behavior, particularly among younger populations (Bandura et al. 1996; Pelton et al. 2004), and these studies are primarily concerned with hostile or belligerent behaviors and attitudes. For example, studies have examined how participants employed moral disengagement strategies to express hostility and support of military force following the 9/11 attacks (Aquino, Reed, Thau, and Freeman 2006; McAllister, Bandura, Morrison, and Gussendorf 2003). Another project focused on how viewers morally judged characters' motives and actions in TV crime dramas (Raney and Bryant 2002). More recent research has demonstrated that moral disengagement contributes toward the relationship between enjoying violent media and the frequent consumption of violent media (Richmond and Wilson 2008). Although this research provides a useful framework while suggesting that coping strategies and moral disengagement promote real-world aggression and the enjoyment of fictional media violence, the situation may be significantly more complex when the audience is aware that they are watching real media violence. Is it possible for viewers to still use disengagement strategies to dismiss violence as fake or staged when they know that that they are watching bad things happen to real people—as in the case of the Knockout Game?

DISENGAGEMENT AND ENJOYING REAL MEDIA VIOLENCE

We now know that viewers tend to use rationalization and coping processes when they watch unpleasant content that could threaten overall fictional media enjoyment. Cantor (2002) notes that audiences are generally aware of their physical separation from what they watch on television or in a movie, and therefore "know that it never did happen... [or] never could happen" (291). So we instead engage in a superficial and primarily spectator-based relationship with media content and media characters. We may still enjoy the show and like its characters. We may even care about them and sympathize with them. But this affiliation is characterized by an aesthetic distance, the knowledge that it is not really real. This allows us to appreciate from afar, and then return to our own lives.

Perhaps the closest that most of us get to watching real media violence on a regular basis is sports and reality slapstick humor. Indeed, some competitive high-contact sports are terribly brutal. American football, ice hockey, and rugby are prime examples. Most martial arts also involve a high degree of physical injury. Even sports like soccer and basketball can get pretty vicious when the stakes are high. And we enjoy watching and consuming this violence, even cheering our athletes on as they pummel, strike, and pounce on the opponents. Most viewers do not seem to mind watching boxers and mixed martial art fighters inflict mutual bloody gashes and broken noses upon one another. If you have ever watched a UFC match, you know exactly what I mean. The spectacle of violence may draw occasional groans and cringes from the audience, yet we seldom pause longer than a few minutes to sympathize over a nasty injury. Similarly, the reality slapstick comedy genre is another instance of real media violence. Shows such as MTV's *Jackass* and *America's Funniest Home Videos* serve up incredibly violent fare under the guise of comical mishaps and prank videos, and we lap them up. We may grimace at first, but then laugh at overweight people tumbling down a flight of stairs, giggle when small children learning to ride their bikes slam into trees, and chortle when Johnny Knoxville attempts a skateboard slide only to trip and land on his testicles. How can we enjoy other people's pain? How can real violence be amusing?

The answer may lie in the contexts surrounding these media genres. Let us first examine sports. Professional athletes who undergo rigorous training routines know exactly what to expect when they compete. The soccer and basketball players know that they will be jostled and tripped up. The football, rugby, and hockey players know that they will be tackled and knocked off their feet. Martial artists expect to be punched, kicked, and elbowed by their opponents. This training also entails learning how to endure these physical assaults with minimal bodily injury, such as learning how to fall to the ground or block a punch so as to prevent serious physical harm. In addition, unlike the gladiators of yore, most professional athletes wear extremely sophisticated protective gear that absorbs much of the impact. For the most part, therefore, pro athletes are well armed with the knowledge, equipment, and agility to successfully maneuver frequent attacks on their person. This does not entirely prevent the occurrence of unforeseen nasty accidents, yet it does imply that these expert competitors are well aware of the dangers of their respective sports. Besides, they *choose* to do what they do.

This element of agency and personal choice is the primary difference between other media genres that feature real violence and random Knockout Game attacks. The pranksters on *Jackass* and *America's Funniest Home Videos* opt to place themselves in dangerous and risky situations. Therefore, if and when things ultimately go wrong, who is really to blame? Most of us know better than to risk getting shot into the sky from a gigantic cannon or go swimming with sharks. These daredevils exercise personal agency by opting to put their bodies in dangerous situations. The contestants on reality shows who attempt dizzying feats and aspire to stardom know full well that there could be disastrous consequences, and yet still choose to take the risks. As with the professional athletes who persistently engage in high-contact violent sports, these individuals understand that injury is a foregone conclusion. Broken bones, strained ligaments, and sprained muscles are all part of the game, so to speak. As viewers, do these individuals warrant our sympathy and concern when things go wrong? Truth be told, audiences are far more likely to shake our heads and mutter something along the lines of "that's what you get for putting yourself in that situation." Attributive blame is a safe and reliable disengagement coping strategy to fall back on when we are confronted with sporting injuries and daredevil fiascos. If these individuals suffer misfortunes in the course of their professional capacity, let us not forget that it is entirely their own fault for choosing to engage in these activities in the first place.

However, personal agency seldom applies to the unfortunate targets of pranks and accidents on *America's Funniest Home Videos*. These unwitting individuals who have no clue of impending harm are probably most similar to victims in "happy slapping" and Knockout Game videos. Why is it that most viewers are able to laugh at their mishaps with little regard for the physical and psychological injury? Another disengagement strategy may account for this context. Consider the format of *America's Funniest Home Videos*, *Tosh.O*, and other similar prank-driven television formats. These shows invariably feature an amusing and engaging host. This cheery presenter acts as our guide, introducing us to upcoming content, providing a humorous voiceover for the home videos, and eventually wrapping it up with a couple of sharp witty remarks before shepherding us on to the next video. Next, consider the clips themselves, often posted or submitted by viewers. These videos are typically recorded on amateur devices and seldom contain any contextual information beyond the prank itself. Finally, goofy sound effects and a humorous soundtrack are added to the original video by professional editors. Often, these special effects involve replays of the video clip (or sections of it) in slow motion to allow audiences multiple viewings. All these elements combine to generate a format that is designed to provoke laughter and amusement, with little consideration for the victim's misfortune. The funny music and sound effects are reminiscent of cartoons and early slapstick comedies. The host directs our attention to particular details, "Watch junior's face when his sister opens the door" and thus encourages our gaze toward some aspects of the clip, and away from others. Multiple viewings and replays desensitize us to any shock or discomfort that we may have experienced from the first viewing. And lest we see something that lingers uncomfortably on our retina or conscience, the host is there to cheerily wrap it up and herd us along to the next wacky video. The overall format is thus tailor-made to minimize the consequences of any disturbing content. We are encouraged to shake it off, laugh, and keep moving.

As mentioned earlier, most media genres contain several cues that encourage viewers to activate disengagement strategies in order to experience greater enjoyment. Yet, increasingly in the case of emerging real media formats like Knockout Game and "happy slapping" videos, these cues are missing.

We now know that viewers often need to employ disengagement strategies and cognitive coping processes to enjoy violent and dysphoric media content. Yet there is an important difference between fictional media violence and nonfictional media content, particularly with regard to the affective dispositions that we develop toward media characters. Fictional narratives are strategically designed to evoke empathic reactions to specific characters' misfortunes, through character development and plot. However, nonfictional content such as Knockout Game videos seldom provide corresponding contextual details. Although research on moral disengagement and audience responses to mass media has largely focused on fictional formats, there are two notable exceptions. One study investigated Caucasian audiences' attitudes toward authoritarianism and race in reality crime dramas like *COPS* (Oliver 1996). Results showed that viewers who enjoyed and supported the authoritarianism on these shows were more likely to use cognitive coping strategies to reconstrue and justify authoritative aggression based on the race of the alleged suspect. For the most part, irrespective of the nature or magnitude of the crime, these viewers reported negative evaluations of African American suspects, and favorable evaluations of the white law enforcement officials. A second study analyzed emotional reactions to news narratives (Zillmann and Knobloch 2001). Here, researchers found that news that contained more emotional details evoked greater empathic distress among audiences. Not surprisingly, news reports that contained details of victim pain, injury, and suffering generally aroused more distress than comparatively bland news content. The researchers discovered that emotional reactions to the news were not based on the viewer's assessment of the normative goodness or badness of events. For instance, it was not as though a news story about a missing pet received a stronger emotional response than a report about workers on strike. Instead, emotional responses were linked to the viewer's affective dispositions toward the victims and an evaluation of the apparent deservedness of their misfortune. In other words, as suggested by ADT, viewers were swayed by whether or not the victims seemed responsible, or could be *blamed* for their circumstances. This is an excellent example of how moral disengagement can be a potent coping strategy to dismiss and disregard other people's suffering through a process of rationalizing and retrospectively rejecting information.

We now have a good theoretical background to examine how audiences respond to real media violence in the Knockout Game videos. First, we know that viewers experience emotional responses toward media characters, many of which are prompted by the narrative. Second, we also know that these emotional reactions lead us to empathize more with some characters than others. And finally, we know that moral disengagement and cognitive coping strategies enable us to enjoy disturbing and dysphoric media content. Surprisingly little research has examined emotional responses to user-generated online media that contain real violence, such as "happy slapping" and Knockout Game videos. This sets the stage for the current investigation.

II

How Audiences Respond
to Real Media Violence

Imagine watching a Knockout Game video for the very first time, and the initial confusion as you try to determine what exactly is happening. Then suddenly there is a vicious assault on an unsuspecting victim. Just as abruptly, the attack is ends and the video concludes. How are you likely to process this information? How do you make sense of the content? Perhaps you may even need to watch it more than once to better understand what happened.

Fictional narratives are strategically designed to evoke empathic reactions toward specific characters' misfortunes. But nonfictional media content seldom provides a corresponding wealth of information. So what can we anticipate in terms of how audiences process real media violence? For starters, lacking crucial information about characters and context, it is possible that viewers may rely on pre-existing schemata and stereotypes in order to speedily organize the video content into a familiar format. For example, we may tend to look for patterns that we typically apply to fictional media content. This may involve ascribing attributes and goals to differentiate the good guys from the villains. Following this determination, we may decide that we like the good guys and empathize with them. Our preference for cognitive economy may therefore lead us to fall back on existing cognitive frameworks and speedily decode Knockout Game videos so that we can quickly make sense of it and grasp what is happening. But if viewers do indeed tend to use fictional media schemata to process nonfictional media, does that mean that the emotional responses will be similar in intensity to corresponding emotions toward fictional heroes and villains? And do the same disengagement coping strategies that viewers tend to apply to fictional media also apply to nonfictional media? Then again, perhaps viewers will not use fictional schemata after all, but instead develop new frameworks to cognitively process this information.

These questions propel this project. My goal is to determine how exactly we respond—cognitively and emotionally—to real media violence.

This section consists of several original research experiments that investigated various aspects of this phenomenon. The results of these analyses provide valuable new insight into how audiences process real media violence, and reveal some unexpected findings along the way.

Chapter 4 provides an overview of the research instruments that were used to measure viewer responses. Most researchers will tell you that *what* you measure depends to a large extent on *how* exactly you choose to measure it. This chapter therefore discusses the overall research experiment setup, as well as how exactly the specific research instruments were located and (in some cases) modified in order to provide greater reliability and validity. I also outline the criteria underlying the shortlisting and selection of Knockout Game videos for use in this project.

Chapter 5 focuses specifically on the specific moral disengagement and cognitive coping strategies that research participants used while watching the Knockout Game videos. We see that although disengagement was widely prevalent, some viewers devised intriguing strategies to avoid empathizing with the victims. Ultimately, this study reveals the broad range of cues that contribute to the authenticity of raw Knockout Game videos.

Chapter 6 takes a closer look at realism. Specifically, it investigates whether the presence or absence of pre-viewing disclaimers influence how audiences interpret real media violence. For instance, if you are told that the upcoming media content is real, are you likely to believe it? Similarly, does informing a viewer that upcoming content is fake alter their perception of its realism? How about if no information is provided at all? Finally, to what extent do these interpretations influence empathic distress toward victims of violence? The results of this experiment point toward some interesting conclusions about how participants responded to the manipulation of realism.

In chapter 7, I explore gender differences in how viewers respond to real media violence. Most past research suggests that women tend to be stronger empathizers and frequently experience greater emotional responses to fictional media than men. Do these same patterns hold for real media violence? The fascinating results of this experiment provide some unexpected information, and lead to some important conclusions.

Finally, part III synthesizes the results from all the preceding experiments to provide an overview of how audiences respond to real media violence. This section explores the ways in which this project has expanded our knowledge of cognitive processing, empathic distress, and disengagement. It also highlights why this area of research bears increasing relevance and significance today, and eventually points toward topics for future investigation.

FOUR

Measuring Responses to Real Media Violence

So how do we know how much viewers like a media character? How do we know if they are using disengagement and cognitive coping strategies? How do we know whether or not they enjoy a particular movie or television show? The answer seems obvious: Ask them. For the most part, this is what most social scientific research—and media effects research, in particular—involves. However, measuring the nuances of human thought, attitudes, and feelings relies significantly on self-reported data. It is therefore important for researchers to employ relevant instruments that have a proven track record of reliability and validity.

The first step was to identify specific variables of interest for the various experiments. For the current project, these included an individual's inherent capacity for empathy, trait propensity to morally disengage, trait enjoyment of media violence, empathic distress, and enjoyment of video content. I then outlined a series of research questions pertaining to my overall research agenda, developing hypotheses for those contexts where previous scholarship on these topics permitted me to do so. I now provide an overview of the specific variables of interest, explaining the conceptualization and operationalization of each individual variable.

EMPATHY

One of the main purposes of this research project was to see whether viewers empathized with victims in Knockout Games videos, and specifically to determine the level of empathic concern (also referred to as empathic distress). It was therefore important to first determine whether some viewers were more predisposed to empathize in general than others. To clarify, if later results indicated that some participants scored particularly high on empathic distress, I would need to know whether these people were naturally high empathizers in the first place. I therefore used an instrument that was designed to measure an individual's pre-existing inclination to empathize with others. *Trait Empathic Concern*, that is, a person's inherent tendency to experience feelings of concern toward other people, was measured using Davis's (1980) Empathic Concern and Personal Distress subscales. This fourteen-item questionnaire (meaning that the questionnaire contained fourteen separate questions) measured each item on a seven-point Likert-type scale (see appendix A). A Likert scale basically measures variation by assigning incremental numerical values to a particular variable. In this case, there were seven response options, where one indicated "Strongly disagree," and seven indicated "Strongly agree." Testing indicated that this scale was reliable for the current project (Cronbach's α = .79). Also, per the original instrument, five items were reverse-coded, that is, phrased in the reverse semantic direction. For example, if the first two items stated, "I care about other people's sadness" and "I have tender feelings for those in bad situations," the reverse-coded item would be "I do not feel bad when other people suffer misfortune." These reverse-coded items were useful to detect response bias, such as when lazy or bored participants mindlessly and repeatedly select the same response option in order to quickly complete a questionnaire. The Trait Empathy measure thus provided me with a valuable baseline measure for a participant's pre-existing empathic tendencies. I now required another instrument to collect post-treatment responses.

No existing empathic distress instruments proved suitable for this project, primarily because the few such instruments that do exist are primarily geared for fictional content. Items in these questionnaires thus explicitly evoke fictional elements such as narrative plot, character development, and emotional contexts. These factors are meaningless for emerging media genres such as the Knockout Game that clearly do not subscribe to traditional fictional frameworks. It was thus imperative to cast a wider net beyond conventional media effects research and fictional formats. In the absence of any relevant existing instrument that specifically gauged empathic concern for victims of real media violence, I developed an *Empathic Distress* measure from an adapted version of Mullin and Linz's (1995) Victim Evaluation questionnaire, which basically consists of seven subscales (see appendix A). Three of these were relevant to the current project: (a) Victim Responsibility measured by seven items, (b) Victim Sympathy measured by four items, and (c) Victim Injury measured by six items. However, here I encountered a problem. Although this scale was created to measure empathy toward media characters, it was originally designed to measure attitudes toward (typically female) victims of violent sexual assault. Knockout Games videos do not deal with this manner of assault, and some questions were thus irrelevant for this project. The first two subscales of Mullin and Linz's (1995) Victim Evaluation questionnaire (Victim Sympathy and Victim Injury) were useful because they directly addressed a viewer's concern for the victim's physical and psychological welfare following an assault. I therefore combined them to create a composite Empathic Distress measure. Testing demonstrated the reliability of this composite Empathic Distress measure (Cronbach's α = .88).

However, the Victim Responsibility subscale specifically addressed rape and sexual assault myths, and its items were designed to determine the extent to which viewers were likely to blame a victim for a sexual assault. For instance, sample items included, "How much do you think the victim intended to be abused in order to get sympathy from others?" and "To what extent do you think that the victim must have done something to deserve the abuse she received?" I therefore chose not to include this specific Victim Responsibility subscale in my research. However, a victim's role (or *apparent* responsibility) in any assault is an important factor that influences the extent to which onlookers empathize or experience concern for his/her welfare. It was therefore important to conceptualize and assess a corresponding construct for victims in Knockout Game videos.

Victim Complicity

Imagine that a friend complains about an elderly driver who backed into her brand-new SUV while she was legally parked at the grocery store. Would you be likely to empathize about the damage to her new car? How about if, instead of being legally parked, your friend was speeding through the parking lot at the time that this accident occurred? Would you now be more or less likely to empathize with her? Most of us would agree that the victim was somewhat culpable in her own misfortune (that is, attributive blame) in the second situation, and we are thus likely to empathize less in the second instance. Similarly, it was necessary to determine the extent to which viewers considered victims in Knockout Game attacks to be somehow complicit–and thus responsible–for the assault. If true, this might demonstrate a relationship between blaming the victim and experiencing less empathy.

Given the nature of Knockout Game videos, what would make a victim appear to be responsible? Or at the very least, to deserve the attack? What kinds of video cues might suggest that an attack was genuine rather than staged? To answer some of these questions, I conducted a pilot test to determine how viewers assess realism for this particular genre of real media violence.

First, I collected ten short Knockout Game videos in which victims were set upon and attacked by assailants. The videos contained a mixed set of victims: women, children, elderly men, and adolescents. These videos were then edited and stripped of audio because some clips were accompanied by background music that could potentially influence viewer responses. In order to minimize differences based on victim demographics, I selected three videos in which the victim was a White male adolescent. The rationale for this decision is explained in detail at the end of this chapter. I then developed a modified version of the Victim Evaluation instrument and included a perceived realism measure (details below), both of which had been developed specifically for Knockout Game video clips. At the very end of this short questionnaire, I included two open-ended questions to collect richer qualitative responses on how viewers assessed the realism of "happy slapping" and Knockout Game attacks.

My participants were 105 undergraduate students at a medium-sized university in the Pacific Northwest. They watched the three shortlisted video clips, and filled out the brief questionnaire at the end of each clip. At the end of the third video, and after the students had completed the last questionnaire, I explained the purpose of my project and said that I was trying to understand what made videos such as these seem genuine or staged. We then watched the remaining seven short videos (containing the range of other victims), and I asked my participants to list the clips that they found most and least realistic, respectively. I also asked them to jot down how they evaluated realism in these video attacks, providing the following prompts: "Videos like this seem to be real when . . . " and "Videos like this seem to be fake when. . . ." The detailed results of this pilot test are provided in chapter 5.

But more importantly, the pilot test confirmed my initial suspicions that several items on the original Victim Responsibility subscale did not correlate with other items. I therefore chose to omit this subscale. However, based on participant responses to the two open-ended questions, I was now able to develop a more useful Victim Complicity construct for the upcoming project. This new construct consisted of three questions that were measured on a seven-point Likert-type scale to determine the extent to which the victim was considered to be complicit in his own suffering, including awareness of the impending attack and collusion with the attackers (see appendix A). In other words, realism in Knockout Game videos was assessed based on complicity rather than other types of fictional media realism judgments, such as factual realism, plausibility, and probability. Subsequent testing demonstrated that this Victim Complicity measure was reliable across all three experiment groups: real (Cronbach's $\alpha = .92$), staged (Cronbach's $\alpha = .88$), and control (Cronbach's $\alpha = .9$).

ENJOYING VIOLENCE

Another variable of interest to this project was the extent to which viewers enjoyed (or did not enjoy) watching Knockout Game videos. As with the empathy measures above, this meant that I had to first determine an individual's inherent predisposition for media violence. This information could later demonstrate whether a preference for media violence predisposed some participants to enjoy Knockout Game and "happy slapping" videos. *Enjoyment of violence* was determined using Nabi and Riddle's (2008) two-item measure (see appendix A). Both statements in this scale are assessed on a five-point Likert-type scale (1 = Strongly disagree, 5 = Strongly agree), and testing indicated a strong correlation between the two items (Pearson's $r = 0.69$).

After participants watched the videos, it would be important to find out how much they enjoyed viewing them. I measured *Enjoyment of the Clip* using Raney et al.'s (2009) four-item scale. Statements in this instrument are assessed on a five-point Likert-type scale (1 = Strongly disagree, 5 = Strongly agree) (see appendix A). This enjoyment scale proved to be reliable across all three experiment groups, specifically the Real (Cronbach's α = .89), Staged (Cronbach's α = .92), and Control conditions (Cronbach's α = .93).

PERCEIVED REALISM

Realism is a subjective and tricky construct to measure because what may appear to be completely genuine to one person can seem artificial and fake to another. A secondary goal of this project was to determine how exactly viewers gauge the realism of Knockout Game videos. In other words, why do some attacks seem real and others staged? Or, in line with the Spinozan approach, are all Knockout Game attacks across the board unquestioningly accepted as genuine and true? It was therefore important to measure participants' final evaluations of each video clip for two reasons. First, a realism measure would conclusively demonstrate the extent to which viewers considered these videos to be real versus fake. A secondary factor was that the realism measure could simultaneously serve as a manipulation check. This would also later help me discern the extent to which providing pre-viewing information about a video's authenticity impacted overall perceptions of realism. In some experiments (see chapters 6 and 7), participants were divided into Experiment and Control groups, that attempted to "manipulate" the realism of the Knockout Game videos by providing viewers with information about the content—namely, whether it was real versus staged. The manipulation check would thus allow me to determine the extent to which this directive proved successful, as well as whether subjective realism assessments were influenced by pre-viewing information.

Based on the afore-mentioned pilot test, this *Perceived Realism* measure consisted of a single item ("Based on your responses to the previous question, do you think that this video clip was . . . ") assessed on a 6-point interval scale (1 = totally fake, 2 = fake, 3 = somewhat fake, 4 = somewhat real, 5 = real, 6 = totally real). This measure yielded some interesting relationships with the other variables, as discussed in chapter 6.

FAMILIARITY

Finally, participants were asked whether or not they had seen these videos before. This is important because media desensitization research proves that our emotional responses to media (and violent media, in particular) decrease with repeated exposures. You may have noticed this particularly when watching horror movies (which are never quite as scary the second and third time around) and action movies (the stunts and explosions always seem tamer when you know what to expect). Familiarity with these particular videos could possibly imply diluted emotional responses to the content. So I included a simple yes/no categorical measure, "Have you seen this video clip before?" (0 = No, 1 = Yes) to measure familiarity. I also collected participants' demographic details, specifically their age, ethnicity, and gender to determine whether any patterns emerged based on these variables. Gender, in particular, turned up some rather interesting results, as discussed in chapter 7.

This concludes the overview of variables of interest in the upcoming chapters, including their relevance, conceptualization, and operationalization. The next step was to locate and select Knockout Game videos for the upcoming experiments.

KNOCKOUT GAME VIDEO SELECTION

Although some might assume (or indeed hope) that disturbing real media violence is difficult to locate online, the sad truth is that it was remarkably easy to locate a range of these videos. All content was obtained following a simple search on the video-sharing website YouTube, using the keywords "knockout game." I intentionally limited results only to content that specifically fulfilled the following parameters: it appeared to be filmed by an amateur cameraperson with a cellphone, and it featured an attack on an unsuspecting victim. For instance, videos that appeared to be edited from surveillance cameras were not included because they were not created by the attackers for the purposes of recording and later distributing online. Similarly, search results also revealed a range of prank videos, such as those that featured a distracted or sleepy target receiving a light tap or smack from a prankster who quickly darted off. These were also not included as potential experiment stimuli for two reasons. First, the focus of the video was the victim's response to the slap, that is, their confusion, irritation, or amusement. The purpose was therefore to document the target's reaction, instead of the assault itself. Knockout Game and "happy slapping" videos typically only capture the attack on the victim, and end soon after because the attackers (one of whom is the unseen cameraperson) must quickly flee the scene. A second reason for not including this type of video is that these playful attacks were clearly devoid of blatant brutality. Knockout Game videos are characterized by a sinister and undeniable viciousness, in which the assailants clearly intend to inflict serious harm to victims.

Eventually, I narrowed my choices down to ten short clips in which victims were set upon and attacked by assailants. The average duration of each clip was ten to fifteen seconds, and all videos appeared to be filmed using cellphones, as evidenced by the low resolution and grainy image quality. This initial pool of videos featured a range of victims, including young children, elderly men, and women. The scenes described at the start of chapter 1 are drawn from many of these videos. Additionally, some videos contained no audio, whereas others featured audio or overlaid musical soundtracks added through post-editing. I therefore chose to strip all the videos of audio to ensure consistency, and because background music can influence viewers' emotional responses to media content.

However, a new problem now emerged. The attack and victim details varied significantly from clip to clip. For instance, one video showed an elderly man being beaten and chased off a moving bus, and another depicted the extended beating of a young adolescent male by a group of bullies. Yet another video portrayed a middle-aged woman on the subway who was violently slapped from behind by a tall youth, and a fourth featured a random assault on customers outside a corner store. Some videos involved extended beatings rather than a single blow, and others included children as victims. Prevailing cultural norms might thus lead some to feel more outrage and pity when vulnerable categories such as children, women, and the elderly were attacked. In addition, audiences are likely to feel greater empathic concern for those who are at the receiving end of prolonged savage abuse, compared to victims who are struck just once. These anticipated patterns emerged in pilot test responses. It therefore became apparent that the victim would need to be somewhat "standardized" in final experiment stimuli to ensure relatively consistent responses across the final Knockout Game videos. Since the most frequent victim type was a young white adolescent male (four out of the total ten clips), I shortlisted videos that featured this particular category.

A second important consideration was that in order to later "manipulate" the perceived realism of these videos, it would be necessary to capture a range of apparent authenticity in these filmed attacks. Eventually, I would therefore need one extremely real, one moderately realistic, and one apparently staged Knockout Game video to determine how realism assessments correspond to empathic distress for the victim. This was accomplished by asking pilot test participants to rate all ten video clips based on realism. The most realistic videos featuring white adolescent male victims were that of a street fight (40.8%, N = 76) and a cyclist who was "clotheslined" off his vehicle (10.5%, N = 76) by a pedestrian. The vast majority of these participants concurred that a video that depicted assailants descend on a boy wheeling his bike was the least realistic video clip (95.9%, N = 76). This information thus enabled me to finalize the video clips that would be used in the upcoming experiments. I was now ready to begin investigating how audiences respond to real media violence in Knockout Game videos.

FIVE

Realism, Rationalization, and Rejection

I still remember the first time that I encountered a "happy slapping" video. When visiting with family in London in early 2005, my fifteen-year-old cousin erupted into laughter as he checked a message on his cellphone. It was obviously a video because I could hear the sounds of shouts and screams as he watched it. He continued to chuckle until the video ended, and then called his older brother over to watch it again. I could not resist asking what was so funny, to which he promptly handed me his cellphone and replayed the video. My curious amusement quickly turned into confusion as I tried to figure out what I was watching, and then changed to shocked horror as I finally comprehended the scene: an elderly man dozing on a bus was rudely awakened by a blow to his head, and then chased and beaten by two adolescents to the door of the vehicle, and eventually forced to jump from the moving bus into the street. And then it ended. I sat in stunned silence while my cousin's laughter renewed with this third viewing of the video. Eventually, I found my voice. "Why is that funny?" I asked him. He shrugged his shoulders, "Happy slapping. It's just for a laugh," was all he answered, retrieving his cellphone and replying to the friend who had sent him this video.

Years later, when I decided to research "happy slapping" and real media violence, this same question lingered in the back of my mind. I resolved to uncover how people perceive and respond to this sort of content, and especially how some viewers could consider it amusing. Casual conversations with others about "happy slapping" prompted a range of response. While most people shared my feelings of disgust and outrage, others concluded that it was not really all that bad—that the videos made it look worse than it really was. A small number of friends and colleagues even admitted that some of these videos were funny. The majority of those who had encountered "happy slapping" and Knockout Game videos in the past—or content similar to this format—had received forwarded emails with links to the content. It therefore seemed the obvious choice to substantiate my casual observations with a more intentional qualitative investigation and explore how audiences respond to real media violence in Knockout Game videos.

Past research has demonstrated that people who enjoy watching fictional violent media need to activate cognitive coping mechanisms in order to enjoy this content. More often than not, audiences disregard the realism of the portrayed violence (Bryant and Thompson 2002; Cantor 2002) by reminding themselves that they are watching a fictional representation instead of actual events. Thus, no matter how graphic or intense the onscreen violence, viewers tend to engage in a superficial spectator-based relationship with the media characters in these violent situations. Knockout Game videos, however, are a different animal because audiences cannot insulate themselves in the awareness that it is merely a fictional portrayal. These are videos of real people who get beaten and brutalized with little to no provocation. In addition, this content is not secreted away in the Internet's darkest corners for motivated consumers to consciously seek out. Social networking, public forums, and handy email contact lists make it incredibly easy for individuals to quickly and conveniently disseminate this content to mass audiences. The abundance of unfiltered real violence available on the Internet to consumers of all ages demands that we try and understand more about cognitive processing mechanisms. How exactly do audiences make sense of real media violence? What are people's reactions toward the victims in "happy slapping" and Knockout Game videos? Do viewers who are so accustomed to morally disengaging to enjoy fictional violence apply similar strategies when confronted with real violence?

The goal of this particular study was to examine audiences' cognitive responses to Knockout Game footage, with an emphasis on the role of rationalization and moral disengagement strategies to disregard the victim's suffering and thus minimize empathic concern for this victim. This would provide insight into the applicability of Bandura's moral disengagement strategies in viewer responses to real media violence, as well as the extent to which any other disengagement and coping mechanisms might also be employed by viewers to dismiss Knockout Games as real or fake media violence. My research was motivated by the following two questions:

> RQ1: How do viewers of real media violence use Bandura's moral disengagement strategies to disregard the severity of real media violence?
> RQ2: What additional moral disengagement mechanisms, if any, are employed in viewers' perceived realism evaluations of real media violence?

There is a prevailing assumption that audiences can instinctively discern real from fictional media content. Yet extant research in this area focuses on the realism of *fictional* media. Concepts such as plausibility, probability, and factual realism imply that a fictional representation is somehow measured against its real counterpart. For example, if a cop on a television crime show arrested a suspect without reading the Miranda Warning, I would conclude that this was not a realistic portrayal of a police arrest because a real cop could not do that. The fictional representation lacks factual realism and therefore seems unrealistic. But no prior media research has examined whether viewers extend this same evaluative process to *real* media content, to conclude whether it is genuine or fake. How exactly do we know whether real media violence videos are real or staged? And what cognitive mechanisms do we use to arrive at these conclusions? A final research question sought to explore this overlooked area of media processing:

> RQ3: What criteria do viewers of real media violence rely on to determine whether onscreen assaults are genuine versus staged violent acts?

The next section provides details about the research participants and procedures.

METHOD

Some details of this study have been outlined in the preceding chapter. As an exploratory investigation into the perceived realism of real media violence, this pilot study provided valuable information about specific audio and visual characteristics that contribute to the authenticity of user-generated Knockout Game videos. The details of participants and videos pertaining to this particular study are now provided.

Participants

My participants were 105 undergraduate students at a medium-sized university in the Pacific Northwest. In this study, my goal was to examine how people gauge realism, and also what disengagement and cognitive coping strategies they are likely to use. I was thus more interested in microprocesses that occur at the individual level, rather than aggregate patterns and trends. At this point in the project, I was not interested in age- or gender-based differences in disengagement. Instead, the goal was to identify unique individual responses to real media violence. I therefore did not collect or analyze participants' demographic information. My impetus was directed by other studies that uphold individual differences between viewers as more accurate predictors of emotional responses to media than larger demographic groups and categories (Goldstein 1998;

Oliver et al. 2009). This line of reasoning is explored in greater detail in chapter 7.

Stimuli

In this particular study, I used three short Knockout Game videos that appeared to be filmed using cellphones. The average duration of each clip was ten to fifteen seconds. All three videos have since been removed from YouTube and are no longer available online. I was particularly careful to select these clips based on the relative clarity of the images and consistency in victim appearance (as outlined in chapter 4). Clarity was important—especially for those participants who may have never seen a Knockout Game video before—in order for viewers to grasp and comprehend the sequence of events in each clip. Some of these videos tend to be extremely blurry and difficult to decipher, largely due to the limited resolution of some cellphone cameras, and also because the cameraperson must quickly record the attack and then escape. The three videos used in this study all featured an adolescent white male victim. Although the preceding chapter contained brief descriptions, I now provide richer details of each video's content.

Clip 1 was thirteen seconds long, and had considerably better image resolution than the other two videos. This was the only clip that appeared to have been filmed using a camcorder or other more sophisticated device than a cellphone. The video begins with a shot of an empty driveway and garage. The camera tracks behind a young adolescent boy who is wheeling a bike with a broken front wheel. He is standing astride the bike and walking it around the corner of the garage. As the boy rounds the corner, two other boys carrying large wooden sticks suddenly rush toward him with wild yells. The cyclist shouts in surprise and jumps from his bike, throwing it to the ground as the two armed boys surround the bike and begin to thrash at it with their canes. The cyclist continues to scream as he runs away with flailing arms, all the while followed by an unseen cameraperson. The video then freezes and fades to black.

Although this video may have been an actual attack, the overall effect could be perceived by some as comical, primarily because of the cyclist's reaction: namely, his excessive screams, clumsy movements, and exaggerated arm-waving as he abandons his bike to run away. For this reason, Clip 1 was selected primarily because it seemed to be the least realistic of the three attacks, and was significantly tamer than the explicit violence in the other two videos.

Clip 2 was seven seconds long, and seemed most similar to typical Knockout Game and "happy slapping" videos that one might view online. The image is extremely blurry and shaky at first, but eventually settles to show a street-lit road at night. As viewers, we can see a figure in the foreground with his back toward the camera, wearing dark clothes and a hoodie so that his features are hidden. Apart from this person, the street appears deserted, possibly because it is late at night. The only other movement in the frame is a distant approaching speck, too far away to clearly discern its details. But as it approaches, we see that it is a cyclist riding down the street toward an intersection. He is riding downhill, so the vehicle is moving fast and he seems to be in a hurry to get someplace. He gets closer to the dark pedestrian. Suddenly, when they are almost parallel, the pedestrian lunges at the cyclist with a well-aimed right hook, catching the rider across his neck under the chin. The strength of this blow coupled with the momentum of the moving vehicle send the cyclist flying off his bike and onto the pavement. He sits up and the camera briefly focuses on the cyclist's dazed and disoriented expression as the video freezes and the screen fades to black.

This video contains several hallmarks of the Knockout Game genre, including the relatively poor image quality, brevity of the video, and vicious attack on an unarmed and unsuspecting victim. Although it may be hard to conceive that a seven-second video could contain so much information, that is yet another trademark of "happy slapping" and Knockout Game videos. They are extremely short and painfully brutal because the cameraperson is only interested in capturing the attack itself. Thus there are no establishing shots or other contextual information provided about the situation or characters. The overriding focus is to revel in the sheer viciousness of a random attack and then quickly escape.

The final video, Clip 3 was different from the other stimuli in some important respects. First, at thirty-three seconds, it was considerably longer than the other two videos. The low-resolution camera image settles to show an adolescent boy's face. His eyes are downcast and there appear to be several blue and purple marks on his face, perhaps old bruises. The camera briefly pans down to show that his hands and feet are bound, and then pans back up to his face. An unseen person's hand then reaches in front of the camera and pulls the boy's hoodie over his head, and tugs at the strings. His eyes remain downcast as the hood tightens around his head, thus obscuring his vision. For a second or two, he stands gently swaying. Suddenly, an off-camera fist swings into view and slams the boy on the side of his head. He stumbles and reels from the attack. But before he can actually fall or recover from this punch, another unseen attacker punches him from the other side. It becomes difficult to tell exactly how many assailants are punching this victim as the blows rain down harder and faster. They continue for about fifteen to twenty seconds as the image gradually fades to black.

Among its distinguishing features, the establishing shot of this particular victim before he was hooded allowed the audience to notice some important details such as the bruises and downcast eyes. This tells us that he is no stranger to physical abuse, perhaps also alluding to instances of past violence. He is thus not entirely an unsuspecting and unprepared victim. Second, although the inferior image quality was comparable to Clip 2, this was the only video that directly focused on the victim's face for the entire duration of the attack. Viewers could therefore witness his (partially uncovered) expression and body language during the assault. The duration of this video also distinguishes it from traditional Knockout Game videos because the victim is continually beaten for approximately half of the total video duration. Indeed, this beating continues as the video fades out. Together, these features make the extended attack on the incapacitated victim in Clip 3 more likely to elicit an emotional response (perhaps even sympathy) from the audience. Unlike the other clips, we have enough time to process and comprehend the savage assault. This particular video thus offered an opportunity to explore differences in emotional responses and disengagement, if any, to a prolonged attack versus a brief assault (Clip 2).

As mentioned above, all three videos have since been removed from YouTube and are no longer available online. However, their apparent "popularity," as evidenced by the number of views registered when last accessed online in June, 2010, were respectively: 5,839 for Clip 1; 12,450 for Clip 2; and 11,386 for Clip 3.

Procedure

When my participants showed up for this study, I first explained to them that they would watch three brief cellphone videos and complete a short questionnaire after each clip. It was important that I did not pre-condition or sensitize them to the content, or risk triggering any pre-existing coping schematas. So I did not provide any other information about the nature of this study or the stimuli at the beginning. I hoped that this precaution would distill their natural cognitive and affective responses to these Knockout Game videos. This is because I was interested in their initial and spontaneous reactions to the stimuli, rather than disengagement and coping strategies that have been pre-conditioned by prank reality TV shows.

Participants then watched the three video clips and filled out the brief questionnaire at the end of each clip. After I had collected the questionnaire for the third video, I explained the purpose of this study and the larger research project, informing them that my goal was to understand what made videos such as these seem genuine versus staged. I then screened more Knockout Game videos (containing the range of other victims detailed in chapter 4) and handed out the second half of the questionnaire that pertained to RQ3. Since most videos were extremely short and of relatively poor image quality, each clip was screened twice to provide viewers the opportunity to fully grasp the recorded attack. Participants were asked to list the clips that they considered to be the most and least realistic, and briefly explain how exactly they assessed the realism of these videos. After this, I thanked them for their participation and answered any questions that they had about the project, the stimuli, and this research study.

Measures

As mentioned, a goal of this pilot investigation was to develop a sub-scale for use in a later study that would measure a victim's apparent culpability in a Knockout Game assault. No existing instrument adequately addressed this particular dynamic, and the closest relevant measure specifically focused on the extent to which rape victims could be blamed for sexual assaults. I therefore developed a brief questionnaire that participants would use to assess perceived realism after viewing each of the three shortlisted video clips, consisting of three categorical questions (0 = no, 1 = yes) that addressed the victim's awareness of the impending attack: "Do you think the victim knew the attacker(s)?" "Do you think the victim knew in advance that he was going to be attacked?" and "Do you believe that the victim was a willing participant in the attack?" These items were designed to evaluate a victim's perceived complicity in a Knockout Game assault, and earlier testing indicated that they demonstrated strong reliability (α = .85). A fourth question measured on a six-point Likert scale asked viewers to indicate the extent to which each clip seemed to be genuine or fake violence: "Do you think that this video was real or fake?" (1 = absolutely fake; 2 = fake; 3 = somewhat fake; 4 = somewhat real; 5 = real; 6 = absolutely real). This was followed by a final open-ended question, with space provided for a brief written response: "Please explain your choice for the preceding question (for example, This video was somewhat real because . . .)." Participants filled out a brief questionnaire for each of the three shortlisted videos.

Once they had completed the third questionnaire, they watched the remaining seven Knockout Game video clips that featured a range of victims—including women, children, and the elderly—that were not shortlisted because they could potentially cause variance based on victim demographics. They then answered two final open-ended questions on realism assessment: "Videos like this seem to be real when . . ." and "Videos like this seem to be fake when. . . ." Although these attacks featuring varied victims could compromise results in the primary investigation, they were included in the second half of the questionnaire to determine overall responses to this subgenre as a whole. There is little evidence to suggest that Knockout Game attackers consistently target a particular victim, even though some attacks have been racially motivated. It was therefore important for participants to watch a range of videos that captured the breadth of violent content and victim characteristics (irrespective of age, gender, and ethnicity) in order for them to determine qualifying attributes that contributed to the authenticity of a Knockout Game video.

Analysis

I enlisted the help of a colleague to qualitatively code the open-ended responses, and thereby minimize researcher bias by demonstrating the validity of this qualitative analysis. We began by looking at those responses that scored low on the 6-point perceived realism Likert scale, that is, scores of "1" or "2." We then categorized the accompanying written response explaining the low assessment score using Bandura's (2002) moral disengagement typology. We each coded all the low realism score statements individually and then compared results. In cases where our choices conflicted, we discussed why this may have occurred, revisited Bandura's strategies for clarification, and then returned to individually code the disagreements again. We repeated this process until there were no further coding conflicts between us.

We then considered the remaining responses that did not directly reflect Bandura's eight disengagement categories. These comments were then open coded, following Strauss and Corbin's constant comparative method (1998) to generate themes. Constant Comparison allows researchers to identify new themes that emerge from data by looking for recurring patterns. As we identify broad themes and continue to code the data, categories become refined and crystallized through a reflexive analytical process (Lindlof and Taylor 2002).

This entire process was then repeated for responses that scored high on perceived realism, that is, scores of "5" or "6," to determine features that added to the realism of Knockout Game videos. Finally, we combed through the data together one more time to revisit and verify our themes, and ensure that the final categories were distinct with minimal overlap.

The next section provides the results of this qualitative analysis of viewer responses to the Knockout Game videos.

FINDINGS

This research study uncovered several interesting findings, encompassing a range of responses to the stimuli, from blatant disbelief and skepticism to genuine distress and concern for the victim. For the sake of clarity, I have divided these results into two categories based on whether viewers thought that the videos were: (a) fake or staged, or (b) real and unfiltered actual violence. The specific disengagement and cognitive coping strategies involved are described within each of these two categories.

"It Just Looked Totally Fake": Rejecting Realism through Disengagement

The first category examines the reactions of viewers who decided that these Knockout Game videos were not real and therefore labeled the clips as "absolutely fake," "fake," or "somewhat fake." Many of these viewers used some of Bandura's (1999) moral disengagement strategies to disregard and minimize the onscreen violence. This in turn allowed them to feel little concern for the victim of the onscreen attack. In addition to these established strategies, it soon became clear that some viewers were using other disengagement processes that are not included in Bandura's typology. So findings are presented in the order of the first two research questions. We will first look at those responses that reflected Bandura's original disengagement categories, and then turn to comments that drew on other coping and disengagement mechanisms.

"Obviously just some Kids Messing Around with a Camera"

According to Bandura (1999), there are eight moral disengagement mechanisms that function to reconstrue the violent act, minimize or disregard its consequences, or target the victim. Most of the participants who assigned these Knockout Game videos weak realism assessments justified their low ratings by using two specific disengagement strategies: minimizing the consequences of the violence and attributing blame to the victim. It is important to remember that these particular disengagement strategies may be influenced by the specific scope and content in these three videos, and are not indicative of responses to any and all Knockout Game videos. Instead, the specific content of a Knockout Game video may encourage viewers to apply some moral disengagement strategies rather than others. That said, those who rejected the violence in the three videos used in this study as fake or unrealistic tended to either minimize the gravity of the attack or blame the victim for his misery.

A large number of viewers accused the boy who was chased off his bike in Clip 1 of deliberately approaching a dangerous situation (78.1%, n = 105), and an overwhelming majority of participants claimed that the violence in this video was staged (totally fake = 63.8%, fake = 32.4%, n = 105). Comments included observations such as "Totally fake because of the way the victim walked into the situation," "[he] didn't do anything to protect himself," and "[he] didn't try to fight back." These viewers assumed that the attack was staged and the victim was responsible for the ensuing assault (that is, attributive blame) because he intentionally walked into a dangerous situation, and then did not attempt to defend himself from the onslaught.

Other viewers disregarded this attack, saying that it was meaningless and trivial because the boys appeared to be young. One viewer noted that, "It was totally fake, it was a bunch of kids messing around," while another said, "Just looks like kids having fun. Seems staged. Stupid kids," and a third stated, "Totally false. Obviously just some kids messing around with a camera and too much free time on their hands. I used to do stuff like that when I was younger all the time." It is interesting to note that these viewers minimize and make light of the attack in Clip 1 because of the characters' ages. In other words, this violence is inconsequential and not genuine because the perpetrators and victim are "just children." This implies that children cannot be violent and that, even though the other two boys were armed with big sticks, it is not as if anything serious could have really happened. By perceiving the attack on the cyclist and his bike as a childish game, these participants are able to pooh-pooh the violence away. Responses such as these suggest some level of desensitization among media consumers who are probably accustomed to more violent fare. The victim was not physically harmed, and the attack is therefore not realistic.

Other responses claimed that the characters in the video were trying too hard to be comical, and that the attack was therefore not meant to be taken seriously. These reactions were evident in comments such as, "Just kids trying to make others laugh," "This video was totally fake because it had a humorous tone to the clip," and "It looked like a group of middle school kids trying to be funny. Didn't buy it as real at all." Humorous violence is thus not intended to be serious. Audiences who are accustomed to slapstick comedy and reality TV prank shows may be drawing on those schematas to interpret this video clip. If it looks like a prank, then it is not meant to be violent. The underlying assumption here is that humor and violence are mutually exclusive, and cannot be simultaneously present because then it is no longer violence. The prerogative to enjoy humorous violence may lead some individuals to not construe it as violence in the first place, and categorize the content as simply humor—harmless fun and games that are designed to provoke laughter and provide entertainment.

Surprisingly, Clip 3 that depicted the sustained and brutal beating of the hooded boy also prompted responses that suggested attributive blame. But these comments solely blamed the victim for not resisting the assault (4.8%, n = 105), such as "It appeared the victim was a willing participant because he sat there and took it," "he wasn't fighting back when being assaulted," and "Did not seem that resistant to be in that location." His inaction and apparent resignation to the attacker's will was perceived as willingness to be injured, as represented by this response, "The fact that he was not fighting to get free makes him appear willing." This means that the boy's passivity toward his attackers has led these viewers to conclude that he is a willing participant in his own torment, and they choose to interpret this as his complicity in the attack. In a particularly twisted and creative application of disengagement strategies to cope with the disturbing content in this video, these viewers seemed to acknowledge the brutality of the attack, but dismiss its consequences by blaming the victim for giving in and taking it. His lack of resistance was perceived as "[he] appears to be okay with getting hit," and the filmed assault therefore was not actually *real* violence. The attackers are thus absolved of blame because the victim should have tried defending himself and fought back. By a cruel twist of logic, these viewers attribute the brutal attack directly to the victim's submissive stance. Never mind the fact that the boy's hands and feet were bound, as briefly shown in the video before the attack began. The fact that these viewers did not notice—or worse, had chosen to overlook—that this victim was unable to retaliate contributed to the lack of realism of this violent video. Unfortunately, there is no way of knowing whether these viewers did indeed retrospectively ignore visual details that interfered with and contradicted the disengagement strategy. Nevertheless, it is still sad and disturbing that this brutal attack was blamed on the victim.

This subcategory therefore shows us that two of Bandura's (1999) moral disengagement mechanisms were applied by some participants to disregard and reject real media violence. Viewers scoffed that the videos were trivial acts of violence, and some claimed that the victim was actually responsible for not directly resisting the attack. However, as we shall see, some viewers used additional disengagement strategies to cope with and reject the realism of these Knockout Game assaults.

"It Seemed like the Videos Were a Complete Setup"

When not relying on Bandura's strategies to reject these videos as unrealistic, viewers found other ways to disengage and rationalize the violence in these attacks. I have grouped these responses based on the two dominant themes: (a) logical inconsistency and (b) premeditation.

(a) Logical inconsistency. Several participants pointed out logical gaps in Clip 1, and questioned the authenticity of the attack on the boy who abandoned his bicycle to escape the other two boys armed with sticks. Most of these comments typically included evidence to support these apparent logical inconsistencies and thus reject the attack as fake. For example, one viewer said that "There was no front tire on the bike. Why would someone bust a pre-broken bike?" and another claimed that the video was "Totally fake because the victim wasn't even riding the bike, he was walking on it, prepared for being thrown/scared off of it." Comments such as these demonstrate a clear cognitive imperative to provide a rational explanation for why the video is not genuine. It is almost as though these viewers who are so used to rationalizing and mentally picking apart media content on a regular basis have jumped at the chance to do the same for these Knockout Game videos. They search for some flaw, *any* flaw, and having found it they triumphantly flag it as evidence that

they were correct. Their suspicions were right and they have the proof to support it.

Still others said that "[the] attackers could be seen and he still proceeded," which seems a reasonable argument that also hints at attributive blame. After all, why would the boy deliberately walk into an impending attack situation? Possibly because he did not realize that he was the intended target of this attack. Yet these viewers do not think that far ahead, and instead grasp at the first logical inconsistency that comes along as an opportunity to disregard the violence as not real. Another viewer observed that "the attackers didn't attack the victim, only the bike." Here, the apparent logical inconsistency was that the bike was already broken and therefore it made no sense for the attackers to damage it further. And some viewers also stated that the video was fake because the attackers focused their assault on the bike, allowing the victim to escape unharmed. By extension, this implies that vandalism and damage to property are not acts of violence. Real violence consists of actual physical injury to another being. Although they do not appear to have considered it, these viewers have overlooked the fact that the bike was indeed broken before the attack and this incident may have been an attempt to finish off the job, so to speak. Without the entire context of the relationship among these boys and why the attack occurred, it is not possible to know why the other boys specifically targeted the bike. And so because they lack the narrative element (that is conspicuously absent in most non-fictional formats), these audience members draw on fictional schemata to justify their confusion and call "implausibility" on this video. In most fictional media texts, the target of violence is usually a person. And when the target is a material object, there is usually enough narrative development and justification for why the object was damaged or destroyed. For these viewers, therefore, real violence is equated with bodily harm rather than harm to property. They argued that these illogical actions implied that the victim was never intended to be injured in the first place. Drawing on the default processing schema, since the victim was not the primary target and the bike already seemed damaged, the video must be fake. Others suggested that the victim was walking his bike instead of riding it, and this is strange behavior for a cyclist. Again, what these comments fail to infer is that perhaps he was walking the bike *because* it was broken and lacked a front wheel.

Over and over again, we see that viewers who rejected this video on the basis of logical inconsistencies present incomplete and hasty arguments to support their case. In their eagerness to explain away the violence and set their minds at ease, they seize upon the slightest flaw to disregard real media violence.

We also see how some participants used pre-existing schemata to ridicule the victim's reaction to the violence, and thus conclude that the video was fake. These comments took on an almost accusatory tone, such as "He ran away really funny almost like acting," "he ran away like a chicken with its head cut off," "the way he ran was comical, he didn't really seem scared," and "he ran off waving his arms in the air in a very comical way. He did not react very fast." These remarks imply that the victim's behavior violated expected and conventional behavior within the given context, namely, violent assault. Drawing on stock representations in narrative formats and pre-existing schemata for how victims respond when attacked, this particular victim's reaction is criticized as being excessive and "over the top," and therefore not realistic. Ridiculing victims inhibits empathizing with them, and thus this is a clear attempt to create a negative disposition toward the victim. By labeling him comical and silly, it is easier to disregard any harm (physical, emotional, or psychological) that he may experience and instead laugh at him.

Interestingly, some participants found ways to question the realism of Clip 2, in which the cyclist is "clotheslined" off his bike by an unseen assailant. These viewers claimed that a lack of adequate and plausible motive on the part of the cameraperson made this video seem fake (fake = 1%, somewhat fake = 7.6%, n = 105) and the violence seem staged. This was apparent in comments such as, "It looks fake and pointless," "why would someone videotape this?" and "why would someone just be standing there with a camera waiting for the guy on the bike to be clotheslined?" These statements are almost indicative of a flailing and confused mind, struggling to come to terms with and rationalize the Knockout Game attack. These viewers do not ask why the attack occurred in the first place, or indeed question the attacker's motives. Their thoughts are clearly not with the victim. Instead, they focus on the unseen cameraperson and claim that the video does not make sense because they can find no clear reason for filming the assault. The violence means nothing in the absence of a narrative to contextualize it. It becomes incomprehensible, perplexing, and devoid of any purpose. This line of reasoning is in direct contrast to an opposite argument in the next section, according to which the fact that these attacks were filmed is direct proof of their realism (see below). In their attempt to rationalize the brutal attack in Clip 2, these viewers have apparently overlooked the sadistic gratification that motivates individuals who perpetrate and circulate Knockout Game videos. It is precisely the decontextualized and arbitrary nature of these violent acts that appeals to the criminals—violence purely for the sake of violence.

(b) Premeditated pranks. Another additional disengagement strategy that some participants used to disregard these videos was that the attacks could not be real because the participants appeared to have planned the event in advance. Viewers who convinced themselves that the victim knew his attacker(s) were also likely to believe that the victim knew in advance that he was going to be attacked (r = .682, p ≤ .01), and that he

was a willing participant in the violence (r = .52, p ≤ .01), as indicated in Table 5.1.

These beliefs were negatively related to assessments of realism, with the victim's assumed complicity detracting most from perceived realism of the violence (r = −.556, p ≤ .01). In other words, those who believed that the victim knew his attackers and was somehow a willing participant in the attack were most likely to rate the videos as unrealistic. Viewers who believed that the victim had prior knowledge of the attack were also extremely likely to think that the victim was a willing participant in the violence (r = .717, p ≤ .01) and reject the realism of the assault (r = −.43, p ≤ .01). These participants argued that the violence was not real because it was premeditated, making the victim and attacker co-conspirators in a staged performance.

This was most evident in the case of Clip 1, where claims that the attack was some sort of premeditated prank in which the victim and attackers were co-conspirators resulted in responses such as, "It seemed like the videos were a complete setup," "The video was very fake because it was being filmed, and it was obvious they were all acting," "It looks to be too planned out," and "[the] camera was right where it needed to be to capture action and the kids were attacking the bike leaving the victim unharmed." For these viewers, this is not a real assault because all participants seem to have been involved in planning, setting up, and performing the event. The attackers and victim were thus co-conspirators. For some, the presence of the camera was itself cause for skepticism, and comments such as "the camera was right where it needed to be" imply that the violence was premeditated and staged. If the mere fact that an attack is recorded using a camera is enough for these viewers to reject the realism of these incidents, that has unsettling implications for empathizing with Knockout Game victims. "Happy slapping" and the Knockout Game are characterized by the perverse urge to not only perpetrate an attack, but also capture it on video. The swift rejection of these videos as fake and unrealistic (maybe precisely because they are disturbing) simply

Table 5.1.   Correlation between Victim Complicity Assessments and Perceived Realism across All Video Clips

	Knew Attacker	Expected Attack	Willing Participant	Perceived Realism
Knew Attacker	1	0.682**	0.520**	−0.399**
Expected Attack		1	0.717**	−0.430**
Willing Participant			1	−0.556**
Perceived Realism				1

**p ≤ .01

because they exist seems a flimsy and feeble cognitive coping attempt. These same comments overlook the fact that the camera may have been conveniently set up in advance for the sole purpose of effectively recording a surprise attack on a victim.

Although most viewers reported higher perceived realism assessments for Clip 2 (mean = 4.74, SD = 0.97) and Clip 3 (mean = 4.56, SD = 1.11) than for Clip 1 (mean = 1.41, SD = 0.6), sporadic comments stated that Clip 2 also appeared to be pre-planned. This included assertions that the cyclist who was knocked down from his bike as he rode down the street expected to be attacked (6.7%, n = 105) and that he was a willing participant in the violence (4.8%, n = 105). For instance, "The guy walking looks kinda fishy almost as if it is set up," and "This video was more realistic but it appeared to be set up with timing and placement of people" implied that the attack itself was inauthentic because the attacker (and cameraperson) appeared to be well positioned to spring out at the victim. In Clip 3, where the bound and hooded adolescent is repeatedly punched by his assailants, responses claimed, "Somewhat fake because victim appeared to be aware that the attack was going to happen" and "Somewhat fake because attacker knew victim." This adolescent boy was considered to be complicit in the attack (41.9%, n = 105) because he appeared to be aware of the impending assault (71.4%, n = 105) and likely knew his attackers (95.2%, n = 105). However, in this case, his apparent complicity did not detract from the perceived realism of the assault (mean = 4.56, SD = 1.11). In other words, even though the boy appeared to know his assailants and likely anticipated the attack, the onscreen violence still appeared to be authentic. Viewers who did give Clip 3 low realism assessments based these evaluations on the victim's yielding acquiescence, which they perceived as complicity in his own torment. These viewers did not consider the passivity and hopelessness that stem from repeated bullying and abuse. Rather, the victim was held accountable because he saw the attack coming and chose not to resist.

We therefore see that participants employed a range of strategies to disengage and cope with the violence in these Knockout Game videos. Although some of these strategies reflected Bandura's (1999) categories, other disengagement mechanisms invoked logical flaws and premeditation to rationalize and reject the realism of these violent assaults. So we now know how audiences employ disengagement to rationalize Knockout Game videos as "not real." The next section explores factors that contribute to the authenticity of real media violence.

"Realistic, Poor Quality Filming Makes it Believable": When Real is Real

The analysis of the open-ended responses for those participants who gave moderate to high realism ratings for these videos indicated that they used three distinct mechanisms to ascertain reality: (1) Production aesthetics; (2) Premeditation and injury to the victim; and (3) The victim's lack of retaliation. These categories are now explored in detail.

Production Aesthetics

Those who believed that the videos were real appeared to use specific video cues to inform their conclusion. These comments, found predominantly in response to Clip 2, focused on the poor image quality of the video, often referring to the recording equipment and its position with respect to the victim. For example, responses such as "this video was real because it looked like it was shot on a camera phone" and "the type of film footage seems from a cellphone" referred to the inferior camera image and corresponding grainy resolution as evidence to support the authenticity of the violent video clip. Therefore, the technology involved in recording and capturing the event is used to guide the perception of realism; quite simply, "the way it was filmed made it appear to be real," or it was real was because the "realistic, poor quality filming makes it believable." Interestingly, other viewers went so far as to argue that the inferior image aesthetics were themselves proof of a pre-planned attack, as in "[the clip] shows a kid tied up getting hit in a poor quality video. The assault was premeditated and the video proves that" and "the quality of the video made it seem like this was a predetermined set-up to brutalize the victim." For some viewers, the fact that these attacks were recorded using cellphones rather than more sophisticated high-resolution devices was direct proof of the reality of the filmed assaults. Cellphones are easy to conceal and are also extremely portable. So it makes sense that if someone was planning to engage in an illegal activity while in a public environment—such as accosting or assaulting an unarmed individual—and also wanted to record the incident, a cellphone would be the most ideal and convenient choice. Although current fifth-generation smartphones and tablets with sophisticated cameras can produce very high-quality images indeed, it is important to remember that this study was conducted a few years ago when smartphones were barely available for mass consumption. At the time that participants provided these comments, there was a distinct quality differential between cellphone cameras and other superior professional recording devices.

Other participants noted that the camera placement was proof of the authenticity of the violence. In direct contradiction to those other viewers in the previous section, for whom the camera positioning made the video seem fake, the very fact that the camera was ideally situated to capture all the action was proof that this attack had been carefully planned in advance. The scene had been scouted and the best position for the camera had been determined prior to the actual assault. These viewers concluded that the very act of recording it was an integral part of the attack itself. For example, one respondent claimed that Clip 2 was real "because of how they think to take their phone out and film at that moment." Other viewers stated that it seemed to be real because of "where the view was from," and because "the camera angles were not so fake." The convenient camera placement indicates to these participants that the violence was pre-planned and the cameraperson was therefore strategically positioned to capture the assault when it occurred.

Another interesting finding was that for some viewers, realism stemmed from the fact that the cameraperson was clearly in league with the attackers. These participants expressed high perceived realism because "the camera [operator] ran away with attacker" and "the video was filming the attacker, not the victim." The cameraperson was therefore in collusion with the attackers, and that this is apparent in the camera angle, its position, and also the primary object of interest—all of which privilege the attacker(s) over the victim. Knockout Game and "happy slapping" videos are therefore distinguished as artifacts that are created by the perpetrators, and not an uninvolved third party or surveillance device. There is a particular malicious intent in the way that these videos are filmed from locations that suggest advance knowledge of the impending attack, as well as the fact that the cameraperson clearly favors and supports the attacker. For these participants, therefore, the placement of the camera proves that the filmed violence is real and not staged.

Finally, some visual production cues—specifically, lighting and setting—enhanced the apparent realism of these videos. Some viewers in this category struggled to apply pre-existing schemata to comprehend the random sequence of violent events. For example, one participant referred to the "dark, creepy atmosphere" of Clip 2, while others affirmed the realism based on "the look and feel—dark night, attacker in all black—gave a mysterious vibe" and "[because] it was dark and the attacker had a hood on." These viewers are clearly trying to make sense of the filmed assault by using pre-existing crime and mystery schemata to interpret the blurred and shadowy images. It is difficult to see what exactly is occurring in many of these videos as a result of the poor image quality, and also because illegal assaults are more likely to occur in darker poorly-lit places. The schemata that these viewers probably use while watching fictional crime dramas and other violent narratives therefore help them to contextualize the apparently random act of violence in Clip 2. With no clear background information or any follow-up details to clarify why it happened, these participants turn to the image itself for answers. So the dark tones and unclear image become *indicative* of suspense, crime, and social deviance. These are symbols with which they are already familiar, and so they use the poor lighting and dark attire to conclude that this incident is like one of the crime drama genre shows. This is an important finding because it is clear evidence that audiences are willing and able to apply fictional media schematas to interpret real world events and people.

Conversely, though, other participants argued that it was "the lack of details that made the clip look totally real" and "I wish there was more reaction after the victim was assaulted. It would give clues as to if the attacker and victim knew each other." So for these viewers, the absence of a coherent plot and well-developed characters contribute to the realism of the violence. The fact that they are unable to apply filmic and fictional schematas to these uncontextualized random violent attacks lends a raw authenticity to the videos. In other words, these Knockout Game videos are not at all like traditional fictional media fare. The fact that it is diffi-cult to see what is going on, that the content is basically nothing more than a vicious attack on someone, and that the viewer is given no addi-tional information about the characters in the video all contribute to make these clips more believable. Real world violence seldom provides the neat narrative solutions that tie up all loose ends. Indeed, more often than not, we are left shocked and upset by random acts of violence that have no explanation. So for some of the participants in this study, fiction-al schematas played an important role in assessing the realism of these videos. High realism came from the ability—or indeed, the inability—to apply pre-existing fictional schemata to comprehend real violence.

Intent to Harm and Victim Injury

Another cue that participants used to rate high perceived realism was that these premeditated attacks targeted unsuspecting and unaware vic-tims, and typically caused extreme physical injury. Particularly for Clip 2, many viewers struggled to explain the attack and establish a possible motive for the attacker who "clotheslined" the cyclist off his bike. Al-though one participant suggested that "the attacker seems to be a drunk person and just attacks whoever comes to him," another said that "it looked like the attacker had done this many times before," and that this was just another assault in a catalog of pre-meditated violence. Yet an-other viewer noted that "the attacker was lingering behind a car waiting for someone to come along . . . [and he] ran away as soon as the victim fell on to the ground." We therefore see that viewers look for clues that this was an established and recurrent pattern of assault—sort of like a serial attacker—rather than a random one-time incident. They notice details that reveal that this particular attacker has developed a certain technique, if you will, to quickly and violently inflict serious harm and then flee. The motive to cause intentional hurt and injury are therefore indicative of the video's realism.

For others, discerning a repetitive pattern was not as important to assess realism as the resolute intent to hurt someone, a lot. It was clear that the attacker was driven by a violent urge to inflict pain, as noted by the viewer who said "this guy just wanted to hurt someone." This partic-ular comment probably comes closest to the frighteningly random nature of Knockout Game attacks. It does not matter *who* the victim is, but just that there is a victim. Period. Another interesting remark suggested that the delivery and efficacy of the blow that hit the cyclist off his vehicle implied military training. This participant remarked that "it looks as if the attacker was planning on hurting a civilian," an observation that may be trying to attribute the unprovoked assault on an innocent and unsuspecting victim to post-traumatic stress syndrome. We again see an attempt to provide a motive for the attacker, in this case a military personnel's cathartic explosion of violence against a random victim.

Many of those who believed that the videos were real expressed serious concern for the victim's injury and suffering, empathizing with his pain and condemning the brutality of the assaults. Viewers were especially sympathetic toward the victims in Clips 2 and 3. Comments such as "looked real because the guy really got tackled off the bike," "looked like it hurt too much," and "it was damaging enough not to be faked" pay particular attention to the severe injuries that the cyclist probably sustained as a result of this attack. For these participants, there is no way that this victim was complicit in the attack because no one would consent to that type of harm. The video therefore appears to be real because the victim could not have willingly participated and was clearly unaware of the impending attack. Several statements attested to this conviction, including "I don't think anyone would be willing to get knocked down that hard," "I don't know anyone who would be willing to participate in that activity," and "no one in their right mind would willingly be knocked off their bike on to the street." There is a clear attempt to acknowledge and condemn the horrible brutality of this unprovoked assault, and these viewers clearly empathize with the victim. Despite the poor image quality and the fact that Clip 2 lasted a mere seven seconds, these participants are concerned for the victim's welfare, claiming that he "looked shocked after the attack," was "in pain" after being "thrown off his bike," and ends up "confused," "in shock," and "seriously injured."

Similar empathic concern characterized comments for Clip 3, and some viewers refused to acknowledge that the hooded boy who was repeatedly punched had willingly participated in his attack. Those who rated high realism openly challenged any assumption of victim complicity with comments such as, "Who would deliberately let themselves get beat up?" "No one would volunteer to have that done to them," and "Who would want that? Why would a person take so many blows to the head?" The brutality and severity of the beating are thus evidence that the video cannot possibly be staged. Some participants drew particular attention to the victim's defeated facial expressions and body language as proof that the violence was real, stating that "[t]he boy looked sad," seemed "like he was . . . sad/ashamed/embarrassed," and "[the] video was real because the victim's emotions seemed too real for it to be fake." Others noticed the "bruising on the cheeks" and the fact that he refused to look directly into the camera before he was hooded, as though "he knows there's nothing he can do about the attacks and that if he resisted, things would only get worse for him." There is a palpable sympathy in these comments for the fate of a condemned and capitulated victim who is resigned to his imminent physical torture. These astute viewers observe that this particular victim has been previously abused and knows exactly what is coming, yet is powerless to prevent it. Some even voiced concern for his psychological well-being following the attack, stating that the experience could very well leave him "messed up" and "emotionally disturbed." These observations are closely connected to the final attribute that participants used to affirm the realism of these Knockout Game videos.

Lack of Retaliation

The last feature that viewers cited as a source of the realism of these videos was that the victims did not (or could not) retaliate against their attackers. In direct contrast to the previous section where some participants indicated low perceived realism by blaming the victims for not trying to defend themselves and fight back, these responses considered the violence to be authentic (and particularly in Clip 3) because of the victim's perceived lack of retaliation. The victim's passivity and acquiescence in the face of his attackers makes this attack genuine because it is more likely to be indicative of real life. Most victims are either overcome with shock or terror when attacked, and very few have the presence of mind and self-defense training to effectively retaliate. More often than not, we are likely to crumble or retreat within ourselves at the time of an assault.

Interestingly, for these viewers, the hooded boy's lack of retaliation did not make him a co-conspirator or even complicit in the attack. Rather, they interpreted this quiet surrender as the result of coercion, the desire to minimize further harm, or a desire for social acceptance. This was apparent in comments such as, "Looks like initiation to a gang. [The] dude looks like he doesn't want to get hit but is willing to take it," and "The kid was getting beat, but he may have volunteered." His passivity was interpreted as indicative of some form of normalized youth social deviance, such as "some sort of gang initiation," "gang ritual," "punishment," or "hazing." The savagery of the violence is thus not debated, but it is contextualized within some form of institutional behavior that makes it both comprehensible and tolerable. Responses stating that it "looks like he doesn't want to get hit but is willing to take it" and "This looked like either a bullying incident, or more likely [a] hazing or initiation type situation that the victim entered into willingly" make the brutal beating a sort of normalized practice that the victim has agreed to suffer in order to achieve some greater goal. A necessary suffering, if you will, because the victim has consented to his own abuse.

Still others suggested that he quietly acquiesced to the beatings because these were preferable to some far worse fate, as in this statement that summarized the victim's helplessness:

> I don't think anyone would volunteer to have this done even though he looks very calm. I think that is because he knows there's nothing he can do about the attacks and that if he resisted, things would only get worse for him.

Although they implicitly assume that this victim is somehow to blame for his situation, it does not detract from the realism of these videos. For these participants, identifying an explanatory framework that accounts for the brutal assault and the victim's surrender helps them to accept the content and thus increases perceived realism. After all, bullying and hazing targets go through this kind of stuff all the time. So therefore, although it is disturbing, it is probably real. It is important to note that this line of thinking is still using disengagement strategies to minimize the outcome of the violence and perhaps even diffusing responsibility for the act among several individuals, including the attacker(s) and victim. The fact remains, however, that it ultimately enhances the realism of the violent video.

Participant responses in this category therefore claimed that the filmed assaults were real based on specific visual production cues, apparent premeditation, and the victim's lack of retaliation. However, these viewers also tended to interpret passive surrender to one's attackers as normalized social deviance, such as juvenile delinquency, bullying, and gang punishment.

To summarize, the analysis found that viewers who rejected the realism of these Knockout Game attacks did so by resorting to attributive blame and minimizing the consequences of the act (Bandura 2002), as well as searching for logical inconsistencies and arguing that the victim was somehow complicit in a pre-planned prank. Yet, others considered the filmed assaults to be real based on production aesthetics, the deliberate intent to cause harm and serious injury, and the victim's disinclination or inability to defend himself. So based on these results, what can we now conclude about how disengagement strategies and perceived realism apply to "happy slapping" and Knockout Game videos?

CONCLUSION

This study provided valuable new information about the range of disengagement strategies that viewers employ to reject the realism of Knockout Game video assaults. Real media violence occupies a hazy realm between fictional violence and the real world. On the one hand, it is both easy and tempting to rely on fictional schemata to make sense of the characters, the situation, and the assault itself. We inherently look for ways in which this attack is similar to or different from familiar movie and television shows to help us cognitively process and emotionally respond to the content. Yet, on the other hand, the sheer randomness and viciousness of these attacks is a disturbing reminder that the real world seldom makes perfect sense, and that the neat narratives that characterize fictional formats are not always applicable to everyday life.

Bandura's (2002) attributive blame and minimizing consequences disengagement mechanisms proved to be common among participants who either blamed the victim or disregarded the violence as "just kids trying to be funny." Additional disengagement strategies—that may be specific only to real media violence—also emerged, as those who rated low perceived realism attempted to prove logical inconsistencies by challenging the plausibility and factual realism of the characters' actions. These voices argued that since the behavior or circumstances were contrived, the video must not be a genuine representation of violence. In this manner, participants rejected the realism of these attacks by applying cognitive coping strategies to disregard the disturbing content as fake, and thus avoid empathizing with the victims.

Yet those viewers who rated high perceived realism gave us a glimpse into the thought processes and cognitions that guided this conclusion. Visual and production cues that are specific to amateur recording devices, and cellphones in particular, were proof enough that the videos were unmistakably images of real attacks. These viewers also concluded that the image resolution and blurry pictures were consistent with portable cellphone cameras that attackers were likely to use to quickly record an assault and then escape. In addition, camera placement was indicative of advance planning to effectively record a premeditated attack at the time of its occurrence. We also saw that those who rated high perceived realism for these videos were likely to empathize with the victim's apparent pain. Yet, in a surprising twist, some of these high empathizers were also likely to rationalize the violence by ascribing it to normalized social deviance. Therefore, although they felt genuine concern for the victim, they ultimately believed that he had exercised personal choice and agency by putting himself in that situation in the first place. At the end of the day, realism is a slippery and ambiguous construct—especially, it would seem—for real media violence. However, the rich qualitative data gleaned from this study have provided much insight into how audiences cognitively respond to Knockout Game videos.

Limitations

Before proceeding further, it is important to acknowledge some of the inherent weaknesses of this study. First and foremost, the findings are restricted by the nature and content of the specific video clips employed. These results may not apply indiscriminately to all Knockout Game videos and real media violence everywhere, although similar trends may emerge depending on the content. These preliminary investigations must be developed by conducting similar projects with other real media violence formats. Second, since my focus is on how audiences perceive and emotionally respond to the *victims* in these videos, realism assessments may thus be indicative of and emphasize this aspect. In reality, it is possible that viewers may use other means (besides the victim) to assess the authenticity of the violence. Responses and findings are likely limited by the specific prompts provided in my questionnaire. Yet, as a new and emerging subgenre of real media violence, there are no existing perceived realism scales for content such as Knockout Game videos. This study therefore sets the stage for others to conceptualize, design, and construct these important instruments and thus facilitate the systematic and long overdue investigation of real media violence.

SIX

This Feeling is Based on Actual Events

We have all watched movies that began with a preface attesting to the narrative's authenticity. A single statement that appears on the screen shortly before the opening scene that states, "This is based on a true story," or "The film you are about to watch is based on actual events," or something to this effect. These powerful words have the potential to radically alter the viewing experience because we now know that this is no fictional scenario concocted by an imaginative screenwriter. Instead, the narrative is grounded in actual history and has its foundation in someone else's lived experiences. In other words, these media characters portray real people's lives. Now think back to a particularly memorable movie you have watched that was based on a true story. Were there any significant differences in how you felt about these characters, compared to those in purely fictional films? Perhaps an inspirational narrative prompted a greater sense of awe and respect for the human capacity to prevail against challenging odds. Perhaps you shuddered inwardly during particularly chilling crime stories, disgusted and morbidly fascinated by mankind's capacity for cruelty and avarice. Perhaps narratives that are grounded in well-known historical events still led you to catch your breath when the assassin's finger lingers on the trigger ahead of a perfect fatal shot, or when the space shuttle loses its sole communication channel with ground control, or when the abandoned soldiers realize that the rescue unit will not be coming for them after all. Maybe you felt a strong personal connection to the cancer patient, knowing that her struggle bears a striking similarity to that of a loved one. After all, if it happened to these characters, couldn't it just as easily happen to you, too?

By contrast, another more frequent disclaimer often appears toward the very end of the final credits. "All characters and events in this movie are fictional. Any resemblance to actual persons, living or dead, is purely coincidental," or other words along these lines. This reassuring information reminds us that the preceding content was pure fiction, that none of it really happened. Any lingering anxiety or concern for the characters' welfare, or any doubts as to the veracity of portrayed events can therefore be cheerfully abandoned. The sensitive viewer who is still recovering from a particularly realistic and harrowing prison escape that cost several inmates their lives need no longer worry himself about their fate, because neither the prisoners, the wardens, nor indeed the prison itself ever existed. Whether or not you are one of those people who has ever breathed a silent sigh of relief when you see this disclaimer, or perhaps even felt a twinge of remorse that this exciting story has no real world counterpart, it cannot be denied that these simple statements have the ability to influence our media responses to a greater or lesser extent. As movie-telling devices, they are potent and manipulative tools that filmmakers can deploy to arouse deep-seated and meaningful reactions among audiences. This is why filmmakers Joel and Ethan Coen came under fire when it was discovered that the cult movie *Fargo,* which claimed to be based on real events, was not actually true after all (Maslin 2014).

Yet all these observations concern fictional content or the dramatic retelling of actual past events. Increasingly desensitized audiences who are reluctant to empathize with real victims of violence—and for whom fictional schemata and disengagement may be practically second nature—demonstrate creative ways to discount the realism of Knockout Game videos (see chapter 5). So how might one alter these perceptions and encourage them to see that these videos contain images of real pain and suffering? "Just tell them," you might answer, "Remind them that they are watching real violence." This was my next step: to determine whether pre-viewing information influences how we respond to real media violence.

Building on the previous exploratory qualitative study, this second research investigation aimed to determine whether pre-viewing information could influence the perceived realism of Knockout Game video attacks, as well as impact empathic distress toward the victims. We know that a common coping strategy utilized by those who watch violent media content is to disregard the realism by reminding themselves that it is a fictional representation, instead of actual events (Bryant and Thompson 2002). And the preceding study (see chapter 5) demonstrated that viewers evaluated the realism of Knockout Game videos in interesting ways, sometimes using disengagement strategies to convince themselves that the assaults were not authentic. But do audiences inherently discern whether or not a filmed attack is real? Does it matter whether or not they are provided with pre-viewing information that confirms or denies the authenticity of this footage? And how do these evaluations influence any accompanying empathic feelings toward the victims of these violent attacks? This follow-up investigation thus sought to explore these questions and uncover whether or not pre-viewing disclaimers had the ability to influence viewers' emotional reactions to Knockout Game videos.

Previous research has demonstrated support for the Spinozan model of cognitive processing, which states that we comprehend and believe incoming information simultaneously. In other words, our default processing mode is to unquestionably accept all information (fictional or factual) as real at the time of its comprehension. This implies that it does not matter whether we are watching the news, a romantic comedy, a Knockout Game video, or a commercial. During the moments that we watch it, this content is real and true for us; although we may be inclined to retrospectively revisit some of this information and mentally "tag" it as fictional or fake. However, all information is unconditionally accepted as true first, and extra mental effort is required to later reconsider and reject details that have already been processed. This suggests that the participants who considered the Knockout Game videos in the preceding study to be unrealistic and fake actually did more mental work, because they reassessed the realism of these videos in retrospect and decided to "tag" them as staged attacks. According to Gerrig (1993), Green (2004), and Busselle and Bilandzic (2008), most of us do not even consider or evaluate media fictionality unless: (a) something within the text prompts us to do so—such as a narrative inconsistency, factual realism error, or something implausible—or, (b) an external source compels us to question it. Examples of external sources include a researcher's questionnaire or pre-viewing information about the video's authenticity, because they both occur outside the actual media content.

It seems reasonable to assume that telling viewers that a Knockout Game attack is real or staged could therefore lead them to cognitively process the video based on this information. In other words, if the Spinozan model is true, it should be relatively easy to "manipulate" the realism of these videos for audiences. But here we encounter a problem, because some experiments (Green and Brock 2000; Pouliot and Cowen 2007) have demonstrated that realism manipulations in media effects research do not always succeed, and that audiences are sometimes not influenced by pre-viewing information. However, these studies all utilized fictional stimuli and therefore the applicability of these patterns to real media has not yet been established.

So does it matter whether or not you remind audiences that "happy slapping" and Knockout Game videos contain images of real violence? And are they then likely to feel greater empathic concern for the victims? These questions, combined with a lack of previous research on how real media content is cognitively interpreted, led to the creation of the first research question:

RQ1: How does pre-viewing information about authenticity correspond with viewers' realism assessments of real media violence in
Knockout Game videos?

Furthermore, I now also had an opportunity to test the Spinozan model
by examining audiences' default processing mode when they watch raw
and unfiltered media violence. Despite the Spinozan proposition that
viewers should accept what they watch as true, the previous pilot study
(see chapter 5) suggested that this might not be the case. I therefore
developed two more research questions to investigate cognitive and empathic responses to these same Knockout Game videos when pre-viewing
information is not provided:

RQ2: How do viewers interpret real violence in the absence of prior
information regarding the authenticity of Knockout Game videos?
RQ3: How does this interpretation subsequently influence empathic
distress toward the victims?

Now that I had a clear plan of action, I was ready to proceed with an
experiment to discover how audiences respond to real media violence
when pre-viewing information is included.

METHOD

Participants

Participants were recruited from junior- and senior-level undergraduate courses at a medium-sized university and received extra credit for
assisting me with this research study. In all, 144 students completed the
experiment (ninety-five female; forty-eight male). Although my participants' ages ranged from eighteen to thirty years, the average age was
twenty years (SD = 2.47). Their ethnicities were as follows: 76.2 percent
Caucasian American, 7.7 percent Asian, 4.2 percent African American, 4.2
percent Caucasian non-American, 3.5 percent Asian American, 2.1 percent Hispanic, and 2.1 percent Other.

Design and Procedure

The study used a post-test only design, meaning that participants only
provided responses once, that is, after they had watched the video stimuli. The experiment was conducted in a small and quiet room that could
accommodate up to two individuals at a time. This was important because sometimes media responses are conditioned by the social viewing
context. You have probably noticed that watching media with a group,
instead of on your own, alters your own behavior to some degree, perhaps to correspond with that of the group. For example, you may laugh a
little louder while watching a comedy, or cheer (or curse) more than

usual while watching a football game. People may be especially hesitant to express feelings of distress and concern for a character if they happen to be among other viewers who do not share these reactions, and particularly if the other viewers find this same content amusing and entertaining. In addition, some disengagement strategies are more likely to occur and be encouraged when in groups. So it was important that one viewer's disengagement or coping strategies did not "contaminate" the rest of my participants, primarily because I was interested in examining the intricacies of cognitive processing and empathic concern for Knockout Game victims. My participants therefore watched the videos at opposite ends of a small room, where they could not see or hear how the other viewer responded to the content. They viewed these videos on laptop computers, to replicate the typical online viewing experience for this particular media genre. Also, although all participants viewed the same three videos, the sequence was randomized to control for an order effect (in which a viewer's responses are the result of the order in which stimuli occur, rather than responses to the stimuli in general).

There were three viewing groups (conditions) based on the realism manipulation, and participants were randomly assigned to one of these groups when they showed up. The Real condition eventually had a total of sixty participants, and the Staged and Control conditions had fifty-four and thirty participants, respectively. These numbers reflect the research agenda of this study. Since the primary goal was to determine whether pre-viewing information had an effect on how viewers cognitively and affectively responded to the Knockout Game videos, I endeavored to maintain similar sample sizes in the Real and Staged groups to facilitate data analysis and comparison of results. However, the main purpose of the Control group was to explore and examine default cognitive processing modes among viewers (RQ2). The size of this group was thus not a major concern. Depending on their randomly assigned group, participants received different pre-viewing information. In the Real condition, the first video was preceded by the following text announcement: "The videos that you are about to watch are recordings of *real* and actual events." Individuals in the Staged condition saw a different announcement: "The videos that you are about to watch are *staged* recordings. They may seem to be real, but they are not." Finally, those who were randomly assigned to the Control condition received no pre-viewing information at all.

As mentioned earlier (see chapter 4), I selected three Knockout Game videos in which the victim was an adolescent White male to ensure consistency across the videos and minimize prompting responses based on the victim's demographic characteristics. As with the preceding study, Clip 1 (thirteen seconds long) featured the boy who abandoned his broken bike when he was set upon by other boys wielding large sticks, and Clip 2 (seven seconds long) depicted the cyclist who was unexpectedly "clotheslined" off his bike by the dark hooded assailant. However, based on viewer responses to stimuli in the preceding study (see chapter 5), I opted to use a different video for Clip 3 and instead chose a clip that portrayed a street fight. In this twelve-second video, two adolescents wearing hoodies appear to be engaged in conversation on a sidewalk. Apparently, things go wrong very quickly, because one boy suddenly lashes out at the other, punching him under the chin and knocking him to the ground. The assailant then bends over the victim and briefly speaks to him before launching into a series of vicious kicks to the victim's face and head. The victim cowers and rolls aside, raising his arms to protect his head. However, this is to no avail and the kicks keep coming. Eventually, the screen fades to black. Although its duration was comparable to the other two videos, this particular video depicted an extended attack on a victim. I intentionally selected this video because I was curious to see if intense and unrelenting assaults elicited greater empathic concern for victims compared to single attacks. These video clips were also strategically selected based on a pilot test to encompass a range of "realistic" violent attacks based on the intensity of the assault. Clips 2 and 3 received high perceived realism ratings, with 40.8 percent (N = 76) of pilot test participants stating that Clip 3 was extremely realistic and 10.5 percent (N = 76) claiming that Clip 2 was very realistic. Clip 1 was overwhelmingly considered to be the least realistic attack, with 95.9 percent (N = 76) of pilot test viewers rating it as very low in perceived realism. This realism variance based on video content was therefore also expected to contribute to the results of this research study.

All three videos have since been removed from YouTube and are no longer available online. However, their apparent "popularity," as evidenced by the number of views registered when last accessed in June, 2010, were, respectively: 5,839 for Clip 1; 12,450 for Clip 2; and 10,539 for Clip 3.

At the end of each clip, participants completed a brief online questionnaire that measured Empathic Distress toward the victim in that particular video (see appendix B). I used two versions of this questionnaire for each viewing condition in which the questions were randomized to minimize an order effect. After they had completed the questionnaire for the third video, participants received a final set of questions that specifically addressed victim complicity and perceived realism. Finally, they were asked if they had seen any of these videos before. None of the participants in this study were familiar with these particular video clips. I then thanked them for their participation, and answered any questions that they had about this study and the videos.

Measures

After each video, participants filled out a brief post-test questionnaire (see appendix B) that was designed to obtain reactions to the clip and the assault victim.

Empathic distress was measured using the adapted version of Mullin and Linz's (1995) Victim Evaluation questionnaire, which consisted of two subscales: (a) Victim Responsibility, Victim Sympathy measured by four items, and (b) Victim Injury measured by six items. The Sympathy and Injury subscales addressed a viewer's concern for the victim's physical and psychological welfare after an assault, and together constituted a composite Empathic Distress measure. This measure demonstrated good reliability across the Real (Cronbach's α = .88), Staged (Cronbach's α = .88), and Control viewing conditions (Cronbach's α = .86).

Victim Complicity. As mentioned (see chapter 4), the Victim Responsibility subscale in Mullin and Linz's (1995) Victim Evaluation questionnaire was replaced by a victim complicity measure, which participants completed at the end of the third video. This consisted of three items measured on a seven-point Likert-type scale that questioned the extent to which the victim was considered to be complicit in the assault and his consequent injury, including awareness of the impending attack and collusion with the attackers. Analysis confirmed the reliability of this measure across the Real (Cronbach's α = .92), Staged (Cronbach's α = .88), and Control conditions (Cronbach's α = .9).

Perceived Realism. This item also appeared at the end of the questionnaire after the third clip, and determined the viewer's final realism evaluation of the three videos. It was developed based on an earlier study (see chapter 5) which indicated that viewers commonly looked for signs of victim complicity when trying to determine whether the violence in these Knockout Game videos is genuine or not. This measure consisted of a single statement ("Based on your responses to the previous question, do you think that this video clip was":) assessed on a six-point interval scale (1 = totally fake, 2 = fake, 3 = somewhat fake, 4 = somewhat real, 5 = real, 6 = totally real). The response was therefore tied to the preceding Victim Complicity questions and indicated the extent to which a Knockout Game attack seemed genuine based on whether or not a victim appeared to be in collusion with his attacker, or had somehow done something to deserve or warrant the attack. Simultaneously, however, this same Perceived Realism measure also served as a manipulation check. This was because it allowed me to determine whether realism assessments were in line with pre-viewing information in the Real and Staged viewing groups.

As expected, this item demonstrated a significant inverse relationship with the Victim Complicity measure for Clip 1 (Pearson's r = $-.61^{**}$, p < .001), Clip 2 (Pearson's r = $-.42^{**}$, p < .001), and Clip 3 (Pearson's r = $-.29^{**}$, p < .001). In other words, the more complicit a victim seemed, the less realistic the attack. We can also see that Clip 1 was perceived as far less realistic than Clip 2 and Clip 3.

Data were analyzed using the SPSS statistical analysis software (Version 17) and demonstrated some interesting results. The next section examines the major findings of this study.

RESULTS

Pre-Viewing Information and Realism Assessment

The first research question attempted to understand the extent to which pre-viewing information about the authenticity of these Knockout Game videos influenced viewers' realism evaluations. I had attempted to create variance in my participants' realism assessments based on the viewing group by either informing them in advance that the videos were genuine (Real condition) or pre-planned and fake (Staged condition), and then see if there were corresponding differences in empathic concern toward the victims.

Analysis indicated that the pre-defined realism manipulation was unsuccessful. This means that the pre-viewing information had no bearing on participants' average perceived realism assessments across the three viewing groups (see Table 6.1 and Figure 6.1).

A follow-up independent samples t-test also confirmed that there were no significant differences in perceived realism across the Real (M = 3.66, SD = 1.70) and Staged (M = 3.94, SD = 1.74) viewing conditions, $t(335)$ = −1.52, p = .129. These findings therefore corroborate earlier research studies in which audiences were not influenced by pre-viewing information (Green and Brock 2000; Pouliot and Cowen 2007). This is interesting because it shows that telling an audience that events are real does not necessarily mean that they accept this information as true.

Table 6.1. Means of Perceived Realism Assessment by Manipulation and Overall

	Real Condition (n = 59)	Staged Condition (n = 54)	Control Condition (n = 30)	Overall
Clip 1	1.90 (SD = 1.09)	2.26 (SD = 1.35)	1.90 (SD = 1.37)	2.03 (SD = 1.26)
Clip 2	4.33 (SD = 1.15)	4.72 (SD = 1.18)	4.86 (SD = 1.13)	4.59 (SD = 1.17)
Clip 3	4.76 (SD = 1.17)	4.87 (SD = 1.26)	4.57 (SD = 1.22)	4.76 (SD = 1.21)

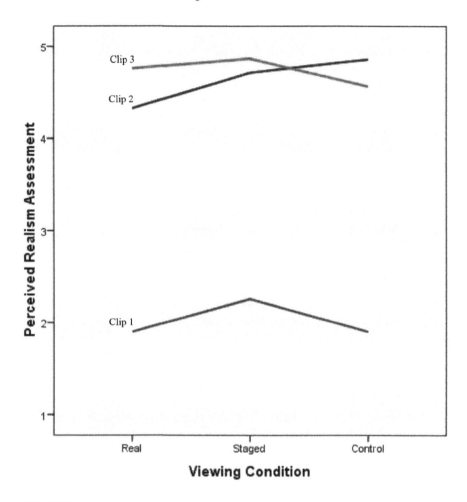

Figure 6.1.

But the data analysis also turned up another intriguing finding. I found that overall realism assessment varied based on the specific Knockout Game video clip. A pattern emerged that was remarkably similar to the pilot test results, where viewers considered Clip 1 to be the least realistic of the three videos. The video of the boy on the broken bike who was chased off by assailants carrying large sticks received a very low average realism rating of just 2.03 (SD = 1.26) on a six-point scale. By contrast, the attack on the cyclist in Clip 2 had a much higher average realism rating of 4.59 (SD = 1.17), and the street fight in Clip 3 where the fallen victim received a flurry of angry kicks to his head also had a high average realism rating of 4.76 (SD = 1.21).

In other words, while the pre-viewing information in each group had no influence on how participants determined the realism of these video attacks, each viewer independently evaluated realism based on a subjective consideration of its content. My participants in the Real and Staged groups either ignored or forgot the pre-viewing disclaimer. Instead, they processed the Knockout Game videos based purely on their own interpretation of the attacks. Even though a participant in the Staged group might have been told that the attacks were all fake, she may very well have rated Clip 1 as "somewhat real," and Clips 2 and 3 as "totally real" because they seemed that way to her. Evaluating and interpreting the very real attacks in Knockout Game and "happy slapping" videos therefore appears to be a subjective assessment that audiences make solely based on the violence that they see with their own eyes, and independent of any pre-viewing or qualifying information.

Default Realism Processing and Empathic Concern

A second aim of this study was to understand the default processing mode for Knockout Game videos, that is, how they respond when they do not receive any qualifying information. This was the purpose of the Control group, whose randomly selected members received no pre-viewing information about the authenticity of these three videos. Their responses would therefore be indicative of the participants' default realism processing mode, and any corresponding empathic concern for the victims in these videos.

Within this Control group, participants reported that Clip 1 was the least realistic violent attack, and it received an average realism rating of 1.90 (SD = 1.37). Interestingly, here Clip 2 proved to be considered the most realistic attack, getting an average realism rating of 4.86 (SD = 1.13). The average realism rating of Clip 3 was slightly lower at 4.57 (SD = 1.22), $F(2, 86) = 51.06$, p = .000, η^2 = .432 (see Table 6.2). For some reason, therefore, the attack on the cyclist who was "clotheslined" off his bike seemed more realistic than the vicious street fight.

As expected, Victim Complicity was inversely related with these realism assessments. A one-way ANOVA confirmed significant differences

Table 6.2. Means of Perceived Realism, Empathic Distress, and Victim Complicity in the Control Group

	Clip 1 (n = 30)	Clip 2 (n = 29)	Clip 3 (n = 30)
Perceived Realism	1.90 (SD = 1.37)	4.86 (SD = 1.13)	4.57 (SD = 1.22)
Victim Complicity	4.88 (SD = 2.39)	1.78 (SD = .96)	3.43 (SD = 1.34)
Empathic Distress	3.66 (SD = 1.81)	5.74 (SD = .87)	5.52 (SD = .93)

among the three videos, $F(2, 87) = 25.72$, p = .000, $\eta^2 = .592$. Viewers in the Control group were not convinced by the boy with the broken cycle in Clip 1 who was frightened off by club-wielding assailants. They were clearly convinced that he either knew his attackers and/or had advance knowledge of the attack, because he received a relatively high average complicity rating of 4.88 (SD = 2.39) out of seven. But the poor cyclist in Clip 2 who was brutally knocked off his speeding bike by the dark pedestrian was considered to be a far less complicit victim, receiving a very low average complicity score of 1.78 (SD = .96). These viewers therefore thought that he was not in any way connected with his assaulter and was clearly an innocent and unsuspecting victim. But in a strange and unexpected finding, the street fight victim in Clip 3 who was felled by a punch and then severely kicked several times received a significantly higher average complicity rating of 3.43 (SD = 1.33). The intensity of the prolonged attack on this boy apparently did not sway viewers who concluded that he was somehow complicit in the attack. Yet this bewildering result may actually be attributable to the specific way in which Victim Complicity was measured, as discussed below.

Finally, as anticipated, Empathic Concern was positively related to Perceived Realism of an attack (Pearson's $r = .519$, p = .000) and negatively related to Victim Complicity judgments (Pearson's $r = -.571$, p = .000) (see Figure 6.2).

This means that viewers experienced greater empathic concern for a victim's welfare when the attack seemed to be realistic, and the victim did not appear to be in collusion with the attackers. In other words, victims who seemed to be genuinely innocent and unprepared when they were attacked received more sympathy from the audience. As visually represented in Figure 6.2, a pattern emerged that clearly mirrored Perceived Realism while inversely juxtaposing Victim Complicity. A follow-up one-way ANOVA confirmed significant differences in Empathic Distress based on the three Knockout Game videos, $F(2, 87) = 24.04$, p = .000, $\eta^2 = .356$. Viewers felt the most sympathy and concern for the unsuspecting cyclist in Clip 2, giving him an average empathic concern score of 5.74 (SD = .87) out of 6. The street fight victim in Clip 3 came next, receiving an average empathic concern score of 5.52 (SD = .93). And viewers evidently did not feel much anxiety or sympathy for the boy with the broken bike in Clip 1, who received the lowest average empathic concern rating of just 3.66 (SD = 1.81).

We therefore see that the pre-viewing information had no impact on realism assessments for any of these videos among the Real and Staged Groups. Instead, audiences chose to evaluate realism subjectively, based on individual realism assessments of each Knockout Game attack. In addition, the default realism processing mode was inversely related to a victim's apparent complicity with his assaulters. Victims who appeared to know their attackers or anticipate the attack in advance led to lower

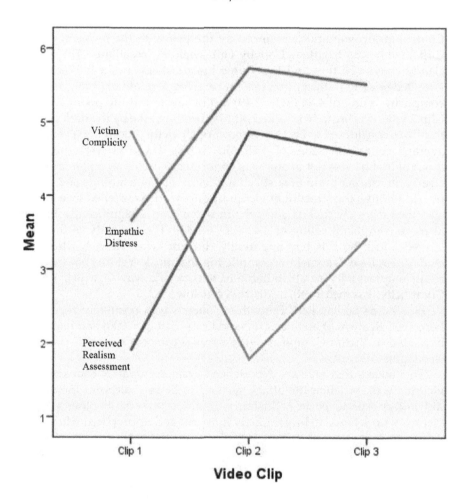

Figure 6.2.

realism assessments, and subsequently gained little sympathy and empathic concern from the audience. By contrast, realistic Knockout Game videos featured victims who appeared to be genuinely unaware of both the imminent attack and their assailants. Audiences demonstrated far greater sympathy and empathic concern for these apparently innocent and unsuspecting victims.

The next section discusses these results in more detail and attempts to explain some of the more perplexing findings.

CONCLUSION

Victim Complicity and Realism Assessment

Realism is a slippery phenomenon, and it is important to recognize that *what we respond to* profoundly impacts any associated affective and emotional reactions. There is a marked difference between how audiences evaluate the realism of a crime drama show, such as *The Killing* or *Bones*, and a Knockout Game video. Although some research has examined the cognitive processing of perceived realism, few studies have focused on real media genres. Research has yet to systematically examine how audiences assess the realism of raw and unedited real media violence, as well as the disengagement strategies that can lead participants to disregard this content as fake and thus reject it.

In order to understand how audiences perceive raw media violence, I attempted to divest them of a popular coping strategy—namely, reminding oneself that screen violence is fictional, a staged and choreographed portrayal of events that never actually occurred. Yet this strategy did not succeed, and my attempt to manipulate viewers' realism assessment did not convince my participants that some videos were real and others were not. Instead, I found that viewers independently evaluated perceived realism and victim complicity, regardless of the pre-viewing information that I provided. This brings us to one of the more puzzling outcomes of this research: Does a seemingly complicit victim diminish the realism of real media violence?

Pilot test participants considered the street fight Knockout Game video (Clip 3) to contain the most realistic violence of the three clips. Viewers also concurred that both this attack and that on the clotheslined cyclist in Clip 2 were very realistic. Yet the street fight victim was also considered to be far more complicit in the brutal and savage beating than the cyclist (see Table 6.2 and Figure 6.2). How can a Knockout Game attack still be considered realistic if the victim appears to be complicit?

In order to understand this apparent inconsistency, it is necessary to revisit the sequence of events in Clip 3. Unlike the other two videos, the street fight clip portrays two males in conversation before one of them strikes the other, knocking him to the ground and then proceeding to repeatedly kick him in the face. Now consider the items used to measure victim complicity: Do the victim and attacker know one another? Did the victim know about the attack before it happened? Was the victim a willing participant in the attack? It seems likely that the victim and his assailant knew one another because they were speaking with each other immediately before the fight broke out. That takes care of the first question. It is also quite possible that this victim knew about the attack before it happened—more precisely, *right* before it happened. The third question is trickier, and some viewers may have interpreted his attempt to fend off the blows rather than retaliate as willingness to suffer. We cannot know for sure. However, based on these three Victim Complicity items, it is not too surprising that they considered this particular victim to be "complicit" in the assault. Nevertheless, the fact that he knew his attacker and possibly anticipated that things were looking south right before the actual fight occurred does not detract from the realism of the savage assault. This explains why an attack can seem realistic and also partly due to the victim's actions. It is clear that this Victim Complicity measure needs more tinkering and refinement so that it is a better indicator of conspiracy and collusion rather than mere acquaintance. There may also be other dimensions yet to be uncovered that also detract from the realism of these disturbing videos.

Perceived Realism and Empathic Concern

It is tempting to explain the inverse relationship between perceived complicity and empathic concern in terms of affective disposition theory (ADT) (Zillmann and Cantor 1976). After all, my results indicate that someone who plays at being a victim but is actually in league with the attackers evokes less empathic concern from the audience. This might suggest that audiences develop a negative moral evaluation toward apparently complicit victims, and therefore experience a corresponding lack of empathy for their plight. To clarify, as a viewer, you would observe the victim's response to the attack, possibly looking for signs of collusion and willing participation. Did it look like they were taken by surprise? Did they seem genuinely shocked and terrified or not? Did they seem to hesitate right before they were attacked, or blindly walk right into it? This reaction would then tell you whether the assault was real and unexpected or staged, and determine how much empathic distress you felt for the victim. Unfortunately, it is not possible to infer any causal conclusions from this study because the realism manipulation did not succeed—which nevertheless brings its own benefits in expanding what we know about perceived realism, as discussed below.

However, it is important to recognize and accept the limitations of applying ADT to Knockout Game videos. This is because ADT has traditionally been employed and developed around affective relationships with characters in TV shows and movie narratives that permit the luxury of complex character development. Audiences thus know who they are expected to sympathize with and who they must root against. Knockout Game videos are vastly different from these traditional media genres. The brief and random nature of these filmed attacks precludes audiences from evaluating and developing affective dispositions with the characters. There is simply not enough time to allow for the traditional ADT process to occur. It is not possible to understand the motives and build an affective response toward the cyclist or his attacker during in the three seconds preceding the brutal blow that knocks the victim off his bike. Nevertheless, several of my participants reported significant empathic concern for these Knockout Game victims. How is this possible? There must be another process that accounts for this empathic response.

An alternate processing mechanism may help explain these affective reactions. Instead of deciding whether or not we like these characters before we empathize with them (as ADT proposes), the characters in these Knockout Game videos are neither liked nor disliked before the assault. Instead, the *violence* differentiates and situates one character as the victim and the other(s) as attacker. In other words, the act of victimization provides all necessary information to interpret this event and discern the villains from the victim. Subsequently, we are likely to feel empathic concern and distress for the unwary target of this attack and (possibly) anger or loathing for the attacker. Therefore, unlike traditional narrative formats, the retrospective analysis of the violent act may be useful to predict empathy for Knockout Game victims. As viewers of these incredibly short violent videos, we may need to reflect and reconstruct the event sequence to understand what just happened, and then develop emotional relationships with the characters (Oatley 1999; Oatley and Gholamain 1997).

To Be(lieve) or Not to Be(lieve)

This study also makes an important contribution toward perceived realism and real media violence. Specifically, it tells us how pre-viewing disclaimers are likely (or *not* likely, in this case) to influence realism assessments of Knockout Game videos. Some research studies that attmepted to manipulate realism through pre-definition have been successful in the past, most notably experiments conducted by Berkowitz and Alioto (1973) and Mendelson and Papacharissi (2007). However, the former employed stimuli that had a distinct narrative structure, and the latter analyzed responses to photographs. Knockout Game videos are a very different media genre because they do not entail an accompanying narrative format. As we have seen, the cues that enable viewers to predict and evaluate reality in media narratives often cannot apply to Knockout Game videos and raw media violence.

My results support and are consistent with past research on perceived realism. Specifically, my failure to manipulate and define the videos' authenticity in two of the viewing conditions underscores the fact that, particularly for this real media genre, realism is a subjective and individual assessment that is independent of pre-defined parameters (see Green and Brock 2000). But that still does not provide an explanation for why these results occurred. If the Spinozan model is correct and the human mind simultaneously comprehends and believes information, why did my participants not accept the pre-viewing disclaimers as true fact and process the videos accordingly?

This leads us to one of the inevitable pitfalls and challenges of most realism research. By default, we are not inclined to consider or evaluate media realism unless something within the narrative or an external source reminds us of it (Gilbert et al. 1990). Interfering with realism evaluation can contaminate or even obstruct it. Therefore drawing attention to realism can potentially backfire, encouraging some people to question and reject it. In other words, by prompting my participants to even contemplate the realism of these Knockout Game video clips before they watched them, I may have inadvertently primed them to pay closer attention to how exactly they assessed realism in the first place. Think about it. If you watched a video that was preceded by a pre-viewing disclaimer about its authenticity, and then you subsequently answered some questions about perceived realism, wouldn't this possibly interfere with how you contemplate and process this video? Perhaps you may now contemplate the video and its minute details in a deeper and more reflective manner than if the researcher had not mentioned realism at all. Or worse, you might become suspicious and engage in skepticism and critical counterargument, challenging and questioning apparent inconsistencies simply because you now suspect that the realism of this content was somehow compromised. Or worse still, you may doubt and second-guess what you watched in the first place, confusing imagination with fact and fabricating memories where none exist. Therefore, informing my participants that the videos were real or staged may have spurred an uncommon interest in this content, perhaps even prompting some to challenge and reject the pre-viewing information by triggering an increased attention to detail.

Limitations

This investigation had its fair share of setbacks. So it is advisable to keep these limitations in mind when considering my results and conclusions. This includes extending major findings to other real media categories, and maybe even other types of Knockout Game videos. The small sample size (N = 144) may have compromised and inhibited statistically significant results and may also explain the low effect sizes (η^2) for some of the ANOVAs. Empathy and perceived realism are very subtle phenomena that may be difficult to adequately gauge in small research pools. Also, in my attempt to ensure similar numbers in the Real (N = 60) and Staged (N = 54) viewing groups, the Control condition only had thirty participants. This investigation and its conclusions could doubtless benefit greatly from more participants.

A second possible limitation regards the nature of the stimuli themselves. Especially for those participants who have never seen a Knockout

Game video, the clips were extremely short, of inferior image quality, and were stripped of background sound and music to avoid conditioning my participant's responses. The unconventional nature of these videos may have made it difficult for these participants to completely understand what was happening in the clips. But then again, this drawback could also be seen as an advantage because while they are still only videos, they mirror the instantaneous, unpredictable, and abrupt nature of real-life attacks. In real life, a random and vicious attack does not give us the opportunity to slow down, rewind, and replay. Instead, we are typically left bewildered and unsettled, wondering if what we just saw actually happened. We often do not know anything about the history and context of those involved in the attack, but are left to form our own interpretations and conclusions. The gritty nature of the video clips used in this study may therefore have simulated (to some extent) real circumstances for those completely unfamiliar with Knockout Game videos and prompted corresponding cognitive and emotional responses.

Finally, it is important to remember that responses toward real media violence cannot be compared or extended to fictional formats. Indeed, it is quite possible that this study may have uncovered very different findings had the victims in the videos been women, elderly people, or children. I therefore caution readers to interpret this study and its findings conservatively, remembering that real violence can occur in many different ways and to many different kinds of victims.

SEVEN

Boys Don't Cry . . . But Do Girls?

Here is Lindsey's idea of the perfect Friday evening. At the end of a long work week, she likes to head home and soak in a nice candlelit hot bath. Then later, she slips into a comfy pair of pajamas, orders Chinese takeout, and sets herself up on her couch with a long cold drink to catch up on all her favorite TV shows from the past week: *The Real Housewives of* wherever, *Revenge, Say Yes to the Dress, Scandal, America's Got Talent, So You Think You Can Dance* . . . you get the idea. Her cats often join her on the couch, snuggling contentedly against her as she flips through the TiVo list to find what to watch next. When she feels like indulging herself, Lindsey may watch one of her favorite romantic comedies or dramatic love stories and laugh (or cry, as the case may be) her way through it. Her well-worn DVD and Blu-Ray collection include such cult classics as *You've Got Mail, My Best Friend's Wedding, Beaches,* and *Terms of Endearment.*

My friend Max's perfect evening, or Saturday, is a whole different picture. He may or may not hit up the gym as he heads home from work. And he may or may not grab a shower when he gets home. But regardless, he will grab a beer from the fridge and throw on a pair of sweats before parking himself on the couch for a long date with his Xbox. Between bouts of *EA Sports UFC,* taking down terrorists in *Sniper Elite III,* and wrestling with demonic forces in *Bound By Flame,* he responds to text messages and calls from Kris and Jake who want to know what pizza topping he wants before they head over. But if the guys don't join him, he's content to grab a bowl of cereal or some ramen and then head back to gaming. Sometimes, he and the others take a break to watch a movie or two. Max's preferences are war dramas, raunchy comedies, gritty action thrillers, and disaster movies. He is particularly partial to sci-fi alien invasion and natural-disaster themed films, although he would abandon those in a heartbeat for the latest superhero blockbuster.

What do you think? Lindsey and Max sound pretty typical, right? Perhaps a little too typical. Maybe even stereotypical: a woman who thrives on romantic dramas and reality TV, and a guy who can't get enough violent combat and loud explosions. Would it surprise you to know that Lindsey is actually Max and vice versa? You are not alone if you answered yes. I was also taken aback when I first realized that Max was addicted to faux reality TV shows and sappy love stories. Likewise, Lindsey's insatiable appetite for mind-defying gaming violence continues to amaze me, and I remember being mildly sickened after she showed off a particularly nifty high-definition maneuver to incapacitate a virtual UFC opponent.

These days more than ever before, we are increasingly reminded that gender is a malleable construct. Traditional gender roles and behaviors—including media consumption—are consistently called into question, despite the fact that some cultural contexts and communities still endorse a rigid demarcation of social responsibilities and norms purely on the basis of gender. Media fare reflects these assumptions, as movies, television shows, and websites develop intentional strategies to attract male and female audiences. But do men and women think and feel differently? Some pop culture commentators and self-help authors would have you think so. But are there demonstrable gender differences in how we cognitively process and emotionally respond to mass media?

Media effects research has a well-established track record of identifying significant gender-based differences in audiences' affective and emotional responses. Consistent with prevailing stereotypes about sensitive and delicate women, female viewers typically report stronger emotional reactions than male viewers (McCauley 1998). Furthermore, women have generally demonstrated greater sensitivity to violence (Cantor 1998; Gerbner, Gross, Signorielli, and Morgan 1980; Riddle, Eyal, Mahood, and Potter 2006), suffering (Guttman 1998; Lachlan and Tamborini 2008; McCauley 1998; Oliver 1993), and empathy (Vollum et al. 2004; Zillmann 1991). Specifically with regard to empathy, past research shows that female viewers are more likely to experience anxiety and concern for media characters' welfare (de Wied, Zillmann, and Orman 1994; Oliver 1993; Zillmann 1991) and report less enjoyment of media violence (Guttman 1998; Lachlan and Tamborini 2008; McCauley 1998). For instance, de Wied et al. (1994) found that female participants experienced more empathic distress toward fictional movie characters in the popular tearjerker *Steel Magnolis*, but yet also reported greater overall enjoyment of the movie than did male participants. Men, on the other hand, tend to prefer and enjoy media violence (Guttman 1998; McCauley 1998).

But these research findings conflict with the earlier descriptions of Lindsey's penchant for violent media fare and Max's decidedly tamer media preferences. So how do we explain those male and female viewers who do not fit these molds? A more recent scholarly trend advocates a nuanced approach to studying media responses, emphasizing the significance of individual differences among viewers rather than broad gender-based conclusions (Goldstein 1998; Oliver and Krakowiak 2009). In other words, these researchers suggest that certain personality traits and characteristics are better predictors of media use and media effects than general demographic qualifiers. As someone who is naturally more empathetic, emotional, and introverted, Max is therefore likely to find that other individuals who share these attributes—regardless of gender—are also likely to share his interests and media preferences. And Lindsey's dynamism and extroversion, mildly flavored with sociopathic tendencies, explain why she enjoys specific media experiences and genres. Rather than think of Max and Lindsey as male and female respectively, these researchers suggest that it is more meaningful to consider them as aggregates of specific personality traits and attributes. Hatfield, Cacioppo, and Rapson (1994) confirm this conclusion:

> According to gender stereotypes, men are less emotional than are women. . . . However, the minute scientists begin to get specific, asking not about one's emotionality but about one's feelings of joy, sadness, and anger—asking not how joyous one is generally, but how joyous one is today—gender differences suddenly begin to disappear. . . . However, there is considerable evidence that women are more comfortable about *expressing* their emotions. [italics added] (142)

This observation supports disposition theories of media enjoyment, which claim that our media responses are both dynamic and unpredictable (Raney 2003), and are influenced by several trait-based factors, including our prevailing mood, interest in a narrative, and attitudes toward particular media genres. Others also note that empathy depends on two factors: the ability to empathize, and one's readiness to do so (Vorderer et al. 2004). Some of us are thus more predisposed to experience and express empathy than others (Detert et al. 2008).

Which of these camps—traditional gender differences or individual differences—holds the answer for how audiences respond to *real* media violence? Given the lack of media scholars' attention to real media violence, it is not surprising that we know next to nothing about how gender predicts differences in empathic concern and moral disengagement toward user-generated violent media content. As suggested by past research, are female viewers more likely to feel concern for victims in these videos? Does gender account for differences in moral disengagement and how much viewers enjoy real media violence? This final study attempts to address this lapse in scholarly literature by exploring these questions. Previous research provides a relatively strong theoretical foundation to advance the following hypotheses:

H1: Female participants will demonstrate greater empathic distress than male participants.
H2: Female participants will demonstrate less enjoyment of real media violence than male participants.

At this point, I would like to briefly clarify that although these hypotheses specifically address outcome variables, that is, people's responses *after* watching Knockout Game stimuli, I resolved to compare these responses with the corresponding trait measures, as well—namely, trait empathy and trait media violence enjoyment. This comparison would demonstrate the extent to which individual differences and personality attributes (rather than demographic categories) predict viewer responses to Knockout Game videos. The next section provides details about the participants, experiment design, and research procedures.

METHOD

The data for this research study were collected simultaneously with those of a previous study (see chapter 6) and therefore several methodological details are similar to those of the other project. This was done to facilitate and optimize research participants' schedules by collecting data pertaining to several variables during a single encounter. Additional surveys were thus administered when collecting other responses to real media violence so as to also investigate gender-based differences. Although the methodology sections below include references to the previous chapter to omit repetitive information, I have included comprehensive details about new measures that relate specifically to this study.

Participants

A total of 144 students who also participated in a previous study (see chapter 6) completed this experiment. Among these, ninety-five were female and forty-eight were male. The average age of these participants was twenty years (SD = 2.47), and they ranged from eighteen to thirty years.

Design and Procedure

This study consisted of a pre- and post-test experiment, in which participants completed an online pre-experiment survey. Approximately two weeks later, they visited a laboratory to complete the second half of the experiment.

Pre-Test

The pre-test instrument was an online survey that was designed to measure personality trait variables. Specifically, in line with the overall research agenda, I asked my participants to complete brief questionnaires that assessed trait empathy and trait media violence enjoyment (see appendix A). Once they had agreed to assist me with this project and signed a participation consent form, I emailed them with a link to the questionnaire. My participants were assured that their responses would be confidential, but I asked them to provide their student ID number in order to accurately link each individual's pre-test with later post-test responses. The student ID number was also used to ensure that they received extra credit for participating in this study.

Post-Test

The post-test data were collected at the same time that participants completed a related research study, and many details are therefore identical (see chapter 6). They viewed three Knockout Game videos on a laptop computer and completed a brief online questionnaire for that particular video at the end of each clip. This instrument measured their Empathic Distress and other affective responses toward the victim of the assault. I also included an Enjoyment measure (details provided below) to specifically measure the extent to which they had enjoyed the content. After the last video, I thanked each participant and answered any questions that they had about this project or the videos.

Stimuli

The Knockout Game videos that were used in this study were the same as those utilized in the previous chapter. Clip 1 (thirteen seconds long) featured the boy wheeling a broken bike who was forced to flee when his bike was attacked by assailants armed with heavy sticks. Clip 2 (seven seconds long) depicted the unsuspecting cyclist who was clotheslined off his bike by the hooded attacker. And Clip 3 (twelve seconds) portrayed the vicious street fight, in which one boy knocked another to the sidewalk before proceeding to repeatedly kick him. Although all three videos are no longer available on YouTube, their apparent "popularity," as evidenced by the number of views registered when last accessed in June 2010, were, respectively: 5,839 for Clip 1; 8,450 for Clip 2; and 10,539 for Clip 3.

Measures

I collected pre-experiment trait measures to later contrast with post-experiment outcome data. In order to avoid pre-sensitizing participants to the research hypotheses, I informed them that the pre-test question-naires focused on perceptions about people and society. This was impor-tant because of the social acceptability and desirability associated with certain personality traits, such as empathic concern. Awareness of the actual goals may have influenced some participants' responses, perhaps prompting them to appear atypically sensitive to others' suffering. After the post-test, however, I clarified the study's actual goals to my partici-pants.

Pre-Test

This online questionnaire was emailed to participants and collected data on the following trait variables.

Trait empathic concern. An individual's inherent empathic concern lev-el was measured using the fourteen items from Davis' (1980) Empathic Concern and Personal Distress subscales (see appendix A). These items measure the extent to which another person's misfortune or pain may cause emotional distress and psychological anxiety. Each statement is assessed on a seven-point Likert-type scale, where 1 indicates "Strongly disagree," and 7 indicates "Strongly agree." Testing demonstrated that this was a reliable instrument (Cronbach's α = .79). As per the original measure, five items on this questionnaire were reverse-coded.

Trait enjoyment of violence was determined using Nabi and Riddle's (2008) two-item measure. This simple and convenient instrument meas-ures the extent to which a person derives pleasure from watching or using violent media. Responses are indicated on a five-point Likert-type scale, where 1 implies "Strongly disagree" and 5 indicates "Strongly agree." Prior testing demonstrated acceptable correlation between both items (Pearson's r = 0.69)

Demographic details. Finally, participants were asked to provide demo-graphic details about their age and gender.

Post-Test

After each video, participants filled out a brief post-test questionnaire (see chapter 6) that measured empathic concern for the assaulted victim using the composite Empathic Distress scale that I developed from Mul-lin and Linz's (1995) Victim Evaluation questionnaire (Cronbach's α = .88). They also stated whether or not they had seen these particular videos before by answering a single categorical item, "Have you seen this video clip before?" (0 = No, 1 = Yes). None of the participants reported seeing any of the three Knockout Game videos prior to this experiment.

Enjoyment of the clip. In addition, participants indicated the extent to which they had enjoyed each video, as well as whether they would be interested in watching other similar videos using a four-item measure

(Raney et al. 2009). Responses to each statement are indicated on a five-point Likert-type scale, where 1 implies "Strongly disagree" and 5 represents "Strongly agree." Again, earlier testing found that this instrument demonstrated robust reliability (Cronbach's α = .92).

Following this, pre-test and post-test data were merged for each participant, and the data were analyzed using the SPSS statistical analysis software application (Version 17). The next section provides an overview of the results.

RESULTS

The results of this study are presented in the order of the two research hypotheses. The first sub-section explores how my participants' gender and empathic concern toward the victims in these videos were associated, and the second sub-section focuses on the extent to which gender was related to the enjoyment of these Knockout Game videos.

Gender and Empathic Distress.

My first hypothesis predicted that, consistent with patterns established by previous media research, female participants would feel greater empathic distress for the victims in these videos than male participants. However, this hypothesis was not supported. No significant correlations emerged between empathic concern and gender, neither in combined responses to all three video clips, nor among responses to each individual video (see Table 7.1).

Similarly, weak and insignificant correlations characterized the combined empathic concern responses for victims across all three videos (Pearson's r = .052, p = .279). Likewise, the correlation between gender and empathic distress remained weak and statistically insignificant for Clip 1 (Pearson's r = .049, p = .558), Clip 2 (Pearson's r = .050, p = .558), and Clip 3 (Pearson's r = .098, p = .243). In other words, regardless of how female participants interpreted the violence in these Knockout Game

Table 7.1.   Correlation between Gender and Empathic Distress for All Videos, Clip 1, Clip 2, and Clip 3

		Empathic Distress – All Videos	Empathic Distress – Clip 1	Empathic Distress – Clip 2	Empathic Distress – Clip 3
Pearson Correlation	Gender	.052	.049*	.050*	.098

$^{***}p < .001,\ ^{**}p < .01,\ ^{*}p < .05$

videos, there was no statistically meaningful association between being a woman and experiencing empathic concern. Gender did not predispose someone to feel more or less empathy for a Knockout Game victim.

I next checked for significant differences between male and female viewers. A one-way ANOVA was conducted on empathic concern responses for each of the three videos, but there were no statistically meaningful differences in the empathic distress reported by female and male viewers for Clip 1 ($F(1, 141) = .35$, p = .558), Clip 2 ($F(1, 140) = .34$, p = .558), and Clip 3 ($F(1, 141) = 1.38$, p = .243). These results therefore contradicted established media effects research that touted women as more sensitive and empathic viewers than men.

However, although gender and empathic concern for Knockout Game victims were not significantly associated, a highly significant relationship emerged between gender and *trait* empathy (Pearson's $r = .352$, p = .000). The pre-experiment data that I had collected on personality traits and attributes demonstrated that women were naturally stronger empathizers than their male counterparts. Similarly, an independent samples t-test revealed that female participants reported significantly higher trait empathy scores ($M = 4.53$, SD = .73) than male participants ($M = 3.97$, SD = .71), $t(141) = 4.42$, p = .000. This means that the women who participated in this experiment were generally more predisposed to empathize with others than were male participants. This specific finding thus complements previous gender-based media research that situates women as more emotional and emotionally expressive than men.

Gender and Enjoyment of Real Media Violence

The second research hypothesis postulated that female participants would enjoy Knockout Game videos less than male participants. Stemming from previous research on male and female media preferences, this seemed to be a logical conclusion. However, analysis revealed that the second hypothesis was also not supported.

Although a weak negative relationship emerged between gender and enjoyment for the combined post-experiment data from all three video clips (Pearson's $r = -.103$, p = .042), this relationship crumbled when I examined reported enjoyment of each clip (see Table 7.2).

Gender was not significantly correlated with enjoyment of the content for Clip 1 (Pearson's $r = -.094$, p = .264), Clip 2 (Pearson's $r = -.119$, p = .159), and Clip 3 (Pearson's $r = -.096$, p = .256). This finding therefore also contradicted established patterns on female media preferences.

Again, one-way ANOVAs confirmed that there were no significant differences in enjoyment between male and female participants for Clip 1 ($F(1, 140) = 1.26$, p = .264), Clip 2 ($F(1, 140) = 2.00$, p = .159), and Clip 3 ($F(1, 141) = 1.30$, p = .256). The second hypothesis was therefore also not supported.

Table 7.2. Correlation between Gender and Enjoyment of the Clip for All Videos, Clip 1, Clip 2, and Clip 3

		Enjoyment – All Videos	Enjoyment – Clip 1	Enjoyment – Clip 2	Enjoyment – Clip 3
Pearson Correlation	Gender	–.103*	–.094	–.119	–.096

*** $p < .001$, ** $p < .01$, * $p < .05$

Puzzled, I turned to the trait measure for enjoyment of media violence. Here, a familiar pattern emerged as the trait variable corroborated established patterns, revealing a robust statistically significant negative correlation between gender and the trait enjoyment of media violence (Pearson's $r = -.290$, $p = .000$). This suggested a statistically meaningful association between being male and liking media violence. Likewise, an independent samples t-test revealed highly significant gender differences in the trait enjoyment of media violence, $t(141) = -3.41$, $p = .001$, with males indicating a greater preference for media violence in general ($M = 2.71$, $SD = 1.00$) than female viewers ($M = 2.13$, $SD = .85$). Male participants therefore did indeed tend to generally enjoy media violence more than their female counterparts.

Therefore, although both hypotheses were proved wrong and there were no gender-based differences in empathic concern or the enjoyment of Knockout Game videos, participants' trait measures clearly aligned with expected gender patterns. Women were higher empathizers than men, and men had a stronger preference for media violence than did women. Why did these patterns emerge in personality trait assessments but not in response to the Knockout Game videos themselves? An intriguing explanation for these results is presented in the final section.

CONCLUSION

An Argument for Individual Differences

This research study has indicated that although gender was significantly associated with trait variables—with female participants registering higher empathy scores, and males indicating a greater preference for violent media—there were no significant gender differences in empathic responses to the video clips or enjoyment of the filmed real violence. At this point, I wish to clarify that this does not imply that there was no absence or lack of empathic distress for the victims in these Knockout Game videos at all. Quite the contrary. Some videos prompted very high empathic concern for the victims among male and female viewers alike.

But there were no statistically significant *differences* in empathic distress and enjoyment purely on the basis of gender. Although this discovery seemingly flies in the face of previous research that has demonstrated strong gender effects, including a female proclivity for empathy (Vollum et al. 2004; Zillmann 1991) and sensitivity to violence (Cantor 1998; Gerbner et al. 1980; Riddle et al. 2006), my results do support more recent investigations that propound individual differences among viewers (Nabi and Riddle 2008; Oliver et al. 2009). Trait variables such as empathy, neuroticism, extraversion, anxiety, and sensation-seeking may indeed be more reliable indicators of how we respond to media rather than blanket demographic categories. Indeed, it is possible that previous research that has uncovered significant gender-based findings may actually be explained by several interacting trait variables, for which gender (in this case) is merely a marker. Cultural grooming, normative behavior, and other socialization processes cultivate and hone certain kinds of attributes and traits among people. As Nabi and Riddle (2008) conclude, "personality traits represent internal factors that affect one's unique life history and social encounters and, therefore, promote chronic construct accessibility" (330). Personal experiences and social encounters thus cultivate specific personality attributes among people. The problem with broad demographic categories is that they run the risk of conferring a static set of characteristics on a given group, anticipating an expected set of behaviors across all contexts. These stereotypes minimize the potential for individual differences, and we thus cannot see the trees for the forest. It therefore may be worthwhile for future researchers to seriously consider personality traits as more useful predictors of human thought and action than demographic characteristics.

The Danger of Words

One of the most puzzling outcomes of this research study was that gender was significantly correlated with trait empathy (Pearson's r = .347, p = .000) and trait enjoyment of media violence (Pearson's r = −.290, p = .000). Yet there were no strong relationships between gender and the outcome measures, specifically empathic concern and enjoyment of the Knockout Game videos. On the surface, these conflicting results make no sense. However, a closer look at the research instruments used to collect this data may hold an explanation.

The subtle wording of statements on these well-established and reliable research instruments insinuates and reflects prevailing socially appropriate behaviors for males and females. In other words, the items on the personality assessment surveys could be considered leading questions in the way that they almost prompt and suggest certain gendered responses. For instance, consider these two statements from the Trait Empathic Concern survey: "I would describe myself as a pretty soft-hearted person," and "When I see someone who badly needs help in an emergency, I go to pieces." Or again, consider this item from the Trait Enjoyment of Violent Media survey: "As far as I am concerned, the more violent a TV show is, the better." Whether intentionally or not, the subtle phrasing of these statements subtly reflects a legacy of socially recognized masculine and feminine normative behaviors. Soft-heartedness and emotional distress, for instance, are traditionally associated with femininity. How many men are likely to respond that they "go to pieces" during an emergency, even if it happened to be true? To do so could risk emasculation, making them seem unmanly. Instead, rebellion, revenge, and an appetite for violence and action are firmly entrenched displays of masculinity. Even women who reflect these particular traits are considered less traditionally feminine, typically earning them masculine labels such as *tomboy*. Several items on the trait-based surveys therefore tap into dominant cultural assumptions about how gender may be performed and enacted. Responses to these items may well reflect an inner desire to self-identify with socially acceptable gender constructions and their accompanying cultural roles (Tajfel and Turner 1979). In other words, it is quite possible that female and male respondents provided information that corroborated and upheld gendered behavior patterns for women and men, and this might explain the distinct gender patterns that emerged among trait variables.

However, the post-experiment outcome measures were quite different in two important regards. First, they require *victim*-centered assessments, rather than evaluations of the self (Heider 1958). In other words, participants were asked to evaluate another person's physical and emotional condition, rather than their own. This may have thus prompted more neutral and objective inferences since the emphasis was on assessing an unrelated third party, rather than constructing an appealing and socially desirable self-image. The element of self-bias was thus conspicuously absent in post-experiment instruments.

Second, the wording of items in the Empathic Distress measure (with the exception of the Victim Sympathy subscale) contain few emotionally laden terms and phrases, and are therefore less likely to encourage gendered responses. To clarify, emotionally suggestive terms in a statement such as "I often have tender, concerned feelings for people less fortunate than me" (Trait Empathic Concern) may prompt some respondents to ponder the gender-based implications of agreeing or disagreeing with this item. For instance, does admitting that he does indeed have "tender and concerned feelings" for other people make a young male less masculine? Items in the Empathic Distress questionnaire instead emphasized a gender-neutral cognitive appraisal of the victim's attack. For example, the question "Do you think that the victim might need psychological help as a result of being assaulted?" is devoid of emotionally suggestive phrases. Responding to this question does not inherently challenge or compromise established self notions of masculinity or femininity because it involves a candid assessment of another human being's welfare. The absence of gender-laced language may thus explain the absence of significant gender differences in post-experiment responses. Instead, this data is indicative of individual differences in empathic concern and enjoyment, irrespective of gender.

If these observations are correct, we do not need to discard any and all established personality trait assessment tools. I am not implying that we should throw out the baby with the bath water. However, I strongly advocate that media researchers pay close attention to the semantic attributes of these research instruments, and prudently and judiciously interpret data that is collected using scales that contain suggestive phraseology, particularly when results reflect significant gender (or indeed, any other sociodemographic category) distinctions. I recommend modifying existing trait measurement scales that do contain these suggestive linguistic elements in order to minimize biased responses.

Limitations

This study shares many of the same weaknesses of the preceding study (see chapter 6) because data were simultaneously collected for both investigations. Among these are the unconventional nature of Knockout Game videos (compared to more conventional media formats) and the sample size. Subtle affective states such as empathic concern may be more observable in a larger research sample. Although 144 participants is not a small number, subtle differences might be observable among larger sample sizes, particularly those that involve a more equitable male-female distribution. Female participants (N = 95) outnumbers male participants (N = 48) in this study, and this may be reflected in the results.

Finally, as with any media effects research, it is important to remember that these results are restricted to this particular subgenre of real media violence. Knockout Game videos specifically feature real footage of unprovoked assaults on unsuspecting victims. I therefore caution against generalizing or extending these findings about gender, enjoyment, and empathic concern to other media genres, including other nonfictional representations of violence.

III

So What?

A former graduate advisor once counseled me about preserving the utility and relevance of social scientific research. "What's the point of it all if it serves no tangible purpose?" he grumbled. "Why go to all the trouble to carefully plan your study, recruit and track participants, spend endless hours sorting and analyzing your data, and preparing detailed follow-up reports if your research does not really help anyone? At the end of it all, so what?" This useful advice continues to ground and motivate much of my research, and provides the rationale for these last two chapters. The all-important "so-what" factor considers the extent to which this project supplements existing scholarly frameworks, while also exploring its broader social utility and implications.

This original research agenda sheds new light on how audiences respond to an ongoing and disturbing manifestation of social deviance. Together, these individual studies address an understudied but promising area of media effects research, and while helping us to understand how people interpret and react to the real media violence in Knockout Game videos. At this point, I would like to remind readers that the bulk of media research continues to focus on fictional formats, examining the design, content, and interpretation of scripted narratives. It is not my intention to belittle these other research arenas, yet it cannot be denied that user-generated real media violence has a particular sociocultural exigency, especially with the opportunities afforded by new media technologies. Images of real people in suffering and pain permeate our media environments with increasing and alarming frequency. While research personnel and funds continue to be devoted to investigating abstract concepts like imagination, presence, social networking trends, and video game decision making, other less examined but nevertheless critical areas are waiting to be explored and chartered.

The final section of this book ponders some of the larger issues implicated by this research agenda. Knowing what we now do about the role of empathic concern, moral disengagement, and coping strategies toward real media violence, what are the next steps?

Chapter 8 situates the major findings and important theoretical contributions of these research studies within their relevant frameworks. These include the role of disengagement and coping strategies in how we respond to real media violence, as well as how perceived realism applies to this genre. I also discuss ADT's shortcomings for examining affective relationships with Knockout Game video characters, and recommend the development of more relevant instruments to effectively measure empathic concern.

Chapter 9 takes these inferences beyond the laboratory to consider this project's macrosocietal implications. Citing several real world instances of how our lives are increasingly permeated by violent images, this concluding essay makes a compelling case for the continued analysis of audience responses to real media violence.

Ultimately, this project provides a springboard to engage a broader discussion on active and engaged citizenry. The Knockout Game, "happy slapping," and their other avatars are ultimately the manifestation of a social sickness. In combatting and addressing this malaise, two significant aspects emerge. On the one hand, an effective response must examine how we (as a society) publicly condemn the twisted minds that perpetrate these attacks. However, on the other hand—and more importantly—this response must also consider the *impact* of these videos on audiences, that is, how we interpret and affectively react to this media content. The contributions of this research project have demonstrated how easily viewers can minimize empathic concern by utilizing disengagement and coping strategies, as well as how apparent perceived realism can impact empathic distress for the victims of violence. Yet these findings are only the metaphorical tip of the iceberg. Much more remains to be uncovered about what we are likely to feel and think the next time we are confronted with real media violence. Will we find ways to ignore, diminish, or forget it? Or will we dare to feel for its victims?

EIGHT

Understanding How We Watch Real Violence

What can we take away from the preceding original research studies? The utility of research lies in its ability to extend the understanding and application of the phenomena under investigation, to add to existing frameworks and theoretical concepts. Much like construction scaffolding, scientific research builds on what has come before, as previous studies provide the foundation to support new investigations that add new levels to existing structures. Occasionally, researchers may use the elevation afforded by these structures to identify new construction sites, uncovering novel and exciting areas for future development and exploration. In the absence of these considerations, scientific research runs the risk of remaining static and isolated, like abandoned little half-constructed silos, that are unable to make meaningful contributions to expand knowledge and understanding.

So what contributions does this project make to its theoretical foundations? If you will indulge my metaphor a little longer, in what ways have I extended pre-existing scaffolding? How do findings corroborate and contrast with what has come before? What potential future construction sites does this project identify? This chapter attempts to answer these questions as I outline the theoretical utility of this research project to media effects research, and also point toward some promising avenues for future investigation.

Although some enthusiastic steps have been taken by media researchers and scholars to explore emerging new media artifacts and usage, these investigations tend to favor content producers. For instance, this research tends to preoccupy itself with users who create blogs, or the intricacies of Facebook and Twitter usage, or online collaborative wikis, or how educators and students navigate online learning platforms (de

Zúñigal, Jung, and Valenzuela 2012; Eyrich, Padman, and Sweetser 2008; Haridakis and Hanson 2009; Raacke and Bonds-Raacke 2008). Few studies systematically explore how this content is received and *interpreted*, particularly with regard to the affective and cognitive aspects of media reception and processing. This research tends to be more interested in why and how often Molly visits a particular website, how many links she forwards to others, how many posts she "likes" on Facebook, and how often she updates her Twitter feed than how others respond to her actions. And those researchers that do embrace media reception typically engage in descriptive analyses of what other users create or post in reply, thus limiting analyses to the never-ending cycle of content production and distribution. Most studies stop short of the messy terrain of cognitive processing and emotional dispositions to online content. Additionally, deviant content is the red-headed stepchild in this overlooked area of media effects research, with very few studies to date that have systematically investigated audience responses to dysphoric and unpleasant online media. Contemporary media effects research is yet to adequately address the explosion of user-generated content in virtual contexts, particularly with regard to the increased availability of unfiltered and uncensored violence. Cellphone videos and other amateur devices allow for the recording and uploading of any content without the supervision, selection, and editing that characterize mainstream media channels. It is therefore imperative for scholars to investigate the darker side of the Internet and Web 2.0, such as increased availability and access to graphic and explicit real violence.

It is my hope that this project will spur increased academic attention to desensitization to violence (Bandura 2002), specifically with regard to non-fictional formats. Using the Knockout Game as an avenue to explore how audiences today make sense of these random disturbing filmed attacks on innocent, unprepared, and unsuspecting victims, I have examined the extent to which prevailing concerns about desensitization apply to audiences' capacity to feel empathic concern for the victims in these videos.

At this point, however, it is also important to acknowledge some of the inherent limitations of my methodology—limitations that no doubt characterize most media effects research conducted in academic settings. First, participants consisted of undergraduate students who were recruited to participate in this research through extra credit and other similar incentives. Although they may constitute one potential audience category for Knockout Game videos, their responses are unlikely to be indicative of other audience categories. In other words, college students are but one of the many potential real-world audiences of Knockout Game and "happy slapping" videos. Furthermore, none of these participants can be said to have voluntarily watched this content, since they were recruited and offered incentives to participate. In this sense, it is important to remember that their responses may not reflect the specific viewer's motivations that characterize those who intentionally seek out real media violence online. A third limitation concerns my focus on isolating and examining *individual* cognitive and affective responses. This imperative influenced the experiment design, in which participants viewed the content individually on a laptop and could not be influenced by others' reactions to the videos. Their responses may thus be very different from the corresponding cognitive and affective processes that typify social group viewing contexts. To clarify, it is quite possible that those who enjoy watching real media violence experience an additional vicarious pleasure from sharing or forwarding it to peers, and perhaps even watching others' reactions to these videos. However, group-viewing contexts entail certain inherent pitfalls, especially with regard to expressing and recording feelings of distress and concern for media characters. The pressure to acquiesce to social norms and conformity can inhibit expressions that deviate from those expressed by the majority. In other words, viewers might likely suppress genuine concern for a media character if it becomes apparent that other viewers do not share these sentiments—and particularly if most other viewers demonstrate hedonically discordant reactions. How likely would you be to express sadness for a maligned character if all your friends hated this character? In addition, some disengagement strategies are more likely to occur and be encouraged among groups. It was therefore important that one viewer's disengagement or coping strategies did not "infect" the rest of my participants, primarily because I was interested in examining the intricacies of perceived realism, disengagement, and empathic concern for Knockout Game victims—and all of these processes are easily disrupted by external sources. Group viewing contexts, while useful to study some of the aforementioned dynamics, would thus have significantly impacted the specific variables of interest in this project. However, examining the nuances of group viewing in online studies with larger sample sizes promises to be a fascinating area for future investigation.

Unlike other well-established media effects traditions that have approached desensitization as habituation and an ever-increasing appetite for more stimulating entertainment (Gerbner et al. 1980), or examined imitative aggression as an outcome of desensitization (Bandura 1965), I chose to focus on its cognitive and affective facets. Specifically, how do contemporary audiences—who are embedded in a media-saturated environment that inundates them with ever-increasing explicit violence—mentally process and emotionally respond to real media violence? When we must invoke disengagement strategies on a regular basis in order to enjoy entertainment media, to what extent does this accessibility and frequent activation diminish our ability to distinguish the fictional from the real? Bandura's (2002) moral disengagement framework proved to be a useful, if not novel, lens through which to examine how audiences selectively reject distressing and disquieting information.

The following sections explore the more significant theoretical contributions and implications of this project in detail. I begin with an overview of how disengagement and coping strategies enabled decreased empathic concern for Knockout Game victims. Following this, I consider how fictional formats and schemata impact the ways in which we respond to real media content, as well as the tenuous yet intricate relationship between perceived realism and empathy for this particular genre of media violence. Finally, I contemplate the inherent challenges of employing irrelevant or linguistically compromised research instruments to measure cognitive and affective media responses, including the extent to which these biased instruments can compromise research findings.

RATIONALIZING REAL VIOLENCE

One of the more interesting and troubling findings of this project was the ease with which disengagement and coping strategies were applied to minimize or reject Knockout Game attacks. This research bridges the largely disparate interdisciplinary spheres of traditional media effects and sociopsychology. Moral disengagement has typically been investigated with regard to ethical agency and behavior (Bandura 2002), and as a basis for the large scale perpetration of inhumanities (Bandura et al. 1996). However, in recent years, scholars have broadened its application to such varied contexts as criminology and the justice system (Osofsky, Bandura, and Zimbardo 2005) and organizational corruption (Moore 2008). Media effects researchers have finally begun to embrace the manner in which moral disengagement may facilitate the enjoyment of video game violence (Hartmann and Vorderer 2009), real and fictional characters in narratives (Krakowiak and Tsay 2011), and anti-hero narratives (Shafer and Raney 2012). Yet this research remains firmly focused on media texts that employ a narrative structure and are (for the most part) lodged in fictional contexts. My project makes an important theoretical contribution by finding a growing middle ground between reality and media representations by exploring how audiences respond to real media violence. By examining the cognitive and affective responses to real media violence, I have drawn connections between cognitive coping strategies and disengagement with regard to inhibiting empathic distress. More importantly, one of the preceding studies specifically showcased a range of creative coping strategies that viewers employed to overlook, minimize, or reject images of real violence. We therefore see the limitations and inadequacies of Bandura's (2002) original typology, as well as how new and emerging media contexts can push viewers to find ever more innovative ways to minimize the dysphoric feelings prompted by unpleasant media content. The application of fictional processing mechanisms to reality suggests the tendency to trivialize and minimize real world brutalities. This theme is explored in detail in the next section.

When confronted with the undeniable violence in Knockout Game videos, an overwhelming number of responses disregarded real violence by resorting to two of Bandura's disengagement strategies: minimizing the consequences of reprehensible acts and attributive blame. Participants found ways to reconstrue the attacks as "just kids messing around" and "stupid pranks," thus trivializing the violence and discursively positioning it as childish behavior. This allowed them to overlook the intensity and sinister motives underlying the assaults, and also brush aside the physical and psychological harm caused to victims. Additionally, we saw that several participants blamed the victim for deliberately approaching a dangerous situation or submitting to the attackers, thereby convincing themselves that the attacks had somehow occurred because the victims *wanted* them to happen. The victims were thus ascribed a masochistic intent that implicates them as abnormal and atypical individuals who do not deserve our sympathy and empathy. Yet, this study also uncovered novel disengagement strategies that reflected the specific characteristics of this particular media format, that is, cellphone videos of real violence. Here, we saw that viewers identified technical and aesthetic production cues that seemingly contradicted and undermined the apparent reality of these attacks. Pouncing upon disparate attributes such as lighting, camera angle, and camera positioning, audience members pronounced that the videos could not be genuine because they appeared to be pre-planned attacks. Arguments such as these betray an almost desperate attempt to locate clues that suggest that these events did not occur. It is almost as though, confronted with brutal images that they would rather not process, these viewers scramble to find ways to discredit the videos and thereby protect their emotional faculties. Similarly, other viewers outlined supposed logical inconsistencies on the part of the attacker, the victim, and overall situation as proof that these videos were obviously staged. Why, they argued, would someone attack another person for no apparent reason? Why would anyone record these incidents? Why would the attacker hit a bike instead of turning on the victim? Why would anyone willingly submit to this kind of abuse and violence? These attempts at critical counterargument, though lacking sufficient grounds and substance, again imply frantic efforts to dispute the existence of these videos and, subsequently, ignore the harsh reality to which they attest. Instead, these viewers prefer to shield themselves from unnecessary emotional distress and concern for an unknown stranger by finding ways to challenge the conceptual and structural features of Knockout Game videos. This coping mechanism may be symptomatic of more sinister psychosocial outcomes of desensitization, such as a disinclination or inability to empathize with distant victims of violence. Further investigation into these and other similar coping mechanisms is required to adequately grasp the scope of their origins and applicability to real-world contexts.

We also witnessed the manner in which some participants, while acknowledging the brutality of the violence in these videos, normalized its occurrence to institutionalized social deviance. These viewers did not attempt to discredit or minimize the violence itself, yet they attributed it to contexts such as bullying and gang punishment. Although not quite attributive blame, this strategy can sometimes dissipate pity for a victim who has somehow done something to encourage the situation or consented to the physical abuse. Normalizing the violence seems to imply a half-hearted resignation and acceptance that some contexts inevitably entail and encourage violent behavior. This in turn situates violence as an unavoidable and inescapable thread in the social fabric. As a disengagement strategy, this thought process rejects the random nature of Knockout Game attacks. Certain situations and groups are inclined to violence, and therefore avoiding them can ensure personal safety. Therefore, here we see an attempt—not to trivialize the violence or blame the victim outright—but instead to deny the chaotic and unpredictable nature of these assaults. Efforts to rationalize and ascribe violence to only particular social spheres suggest a disinclination to unequivocally empathize with victims who encounter violence within those spheres. In other words, the puddle exists, yet most of us would walk around the muddy water rather than dirty our boots by stepping in it.

Perhaps the most troubling and disheartening observation was that indignation, anger, and outright disapproval of the Knockout Game attacks depicted in these videos were conspicuously absent in the viewers' comments. In instances where they did not challenge the realism of these attacks, responses were characterized by a passive consumption of the portrayed events, with little outrage at the fact that they had occurred in the first place. Much remains to be understood with regard to how moral disengagement enables us to reject and disregard real media violence and suffering. This project has outlined some ways in which this process can occur, and I encourage other investigators to further explore these significant social issues.

TRUTH IS STRANGER THAN FICTION

In an attempt to understand how audiences form affective dispositions and empathize with the people in Knockout Game and "happy slapping" videos, I opted to use the media effects theories that seemed most relevant to examining this experience. The paucity of research on real media responses and psychological processing compelled me to use the resources available and determine the extent to which they proved useful.

Affective Disposition Theory (Zillmann and Cantor 1976) seemed most suitable for investigating how moral evaluations of character goals and actions influence the subsequent affective dispositions that audiences form toward media characters. ADT's application has been solely reserved for fictional formats thus far, and (to my knowledge) mine was the first attempt to apply this framework to real and non-fictional media characters. Empathy is an integral component of disposition theory, and stems from the direction of a viewer's dispositional relationship with a given media character. Moral evaluations of a character's actions occur within the narrative framework, where a developing storyline helps us as viewers to understand who this character is and what she desires. We then form subjective evaluations of whether or not we approve of her actions, and consequently decide whether or not we like her. This explains why a protagonist who is driven by noble motives typically elicits a positive moral evaluation and positive dispositions among audience members. Similarly, villains and characters who resort to unworthy actions often evoke negative affective responses. For instance, empathizing with the character Mitchell Pritchett on the popular sitcom *Modern Family* would necessitate that I both understand this character's motives and background, and that I like him. Consequently, I share his joy when his longtime partner accepts his proposal of marriage, and when he and his partner adopt a child together. However, research in this area has been limited to dispositional (and empathic) reactions toward a protagonist within a *fictional* narrative context. We are called upon to activate and access available pre-existing fictional schemata and character models in order to effectively and efficiently process these media characters. Depending on viewing patterns and genre preferences, some schemata and character models are more accessible than others. For example, viewers of historical British domestic dramas such as *Upstairs Downstairs* and *Downton Abbey* are doubtless familiar with such stock characters as the genial and benign aristocrat, the fiercely loyal butler, the knavish scheming footman, the timid maid, and the brusque yet lovable cook. For most of us, our enjoyment of specific genres rests, to some extent, on our ability to identify and apply familiar schemata and character models as we progress through the narrative. This has been pointed out by Tamborini et al. (2009):

> the storylines found in many novels, films and TV programs use formulaic narrative structures and stereotyped characters over and over again . . . [which lead to] the development of plot and character schemas that help audience members understand the narrative and make quick judgments about the characters. (12)

Narratives generally favor heroic protagonists, or anti-heroes as the case may be, and promote identification with this protagonist. Minor characters, including most victims in typical action and violent entertainment media fare, seldom receive more than a cursory acknowledgment. Most of these secondary or lesser characters function peripherally to contextualize the protagonist and bolster his or her character development. In this regard, we seldom pay much attention to these minor characters and may bestow a transient and fleeting token of empathy in their general direction before rushing to catch up with the major characters. Exceptions to this trend include a study in which 48 percent of children who watched a violent television show empathized with the victim, although 45 percent of these same viewers empathized with the violent attacker (Bruce 1995). To some extent, even research on empathic reactions to nonfictional formats, for instance, those that have examined empathy toward victims in news stories and documentaries (Zillmann and Knobloch 2001), relies on some semblance of a narrative sequence to help viewers process the events.

The present study makes an important contribution to this area by investigating dispositional attitudes—namely, empathic concern—toward *real* victims. The video clips were devoid of narrative cues and offered no information to situate the victim as a hero, villain, or unsuspecting passerby. In the absence of a conventional narrative background that provides a foundation for affective relationships with these characters, audiences were encouraged to pay closer attention to the filmed assault in order to comprehend the sequence of events and establish a basis for emotional attachment or repugnance. In this sense, these attitudes may be closer to real world responses toward victims of violence and crimes about whom little contextual information is known. Yet this is exactly why ADT may not be the most appropriate framework to understand empathic responses to real media violence.

ADT has traditionally been employed to understand how viewers develop affective relationships with characters in longer filmic narratives that allow for complex character development. Such plotlines allow us to develop a comprehensive character model for the heroes, villains, and other major characters. Knockout Game videos, however, defy these characteristics and operate very much as fragments of an elusive and fractured hidden larger context. The very nature of these videos, as well as the emphasis on the assault itself and nothing else, robs viewers of the opportunity to determine who exactly these characters are, the nature of the relationship (if any) between them, the reason for the attack, and its outcome. Rather, we witness a brutal assault through the unseen cameraperson's eyes, sometimes struggling to discern details through the hazy and pixelated images. "Happy slapping" and Knockout Game videos do not feature the accompanying voiceover of a helpful news anchor who directs our attention toward specific sections. Apart from the comments posted below these videos on video-sharing websites such as YouTube, there is seldom any information about the contents of the video. Instead, the viewer is left to watch the brutal attack in its stark isolation from background context and figure it out for themselves. In the midst of this arbitrary and chaotic violence that lacks narrative elements, how are we to develop affective dispositions toward characters in the few seconds before they attack or are attacked? While we may struggle to make sense of the incident after the fact, there is simply not enough time to allow for the traditional ADT process to occur. Nevertheless, some participants in this study recorded significant empathic distress for the victims in the videos. If ADT is not entirely applicable, what explains this affective response?

An alternate processing mechanism may be more useful for real media violence and other media contexts that are entirely devoid of traditional narrative features. Contrary to ADT, characters in these videos are not liked or disliked prior to the assault. There is no sophisticated plot and character development to indicate with whom and on whose behalf we are to empathize. Instead, it is the *violent act* that situates one character as the victim and the other(s) as attacker. In other words, the instance of victimization determines whether or not we like the characters in these videos. Subsequently, a viewer may feel empathic concern and distress for the victim and (possibly) anger or loathing toward the attacker. Indeed, we may replay the video to confirm what we just witnessed, and perhaps affirm our suspicions to ourselves. As indicated by some of the open-ended responses, this may explain the presence of certain fictional schemata to the Knockout Game videos. Once the initial surprise and shock have been overcome, we can start to "notice" previously undetected details, as we ascribe helplessness and vulnerability to the victim and devious malevolence to the attacker. Yes, we tell ourselves, this wicked person is driven by sadistic intent and restless depravity to inflict harm on the innocent. Having little else to help make sense of the random violence, our familiar character models and narrative schemata take over as we concoct background stories and "find" details to corroborate these fanciful imaginings. The attacker was hooded, he was wearing dark clothes, and just *looked* suspicious. The retrospective analysis of the violent act—namely, the viewer's reflective construction of the sequence of events—establishes intent, victim, and villain. In this sense, theories that emphasize retrospective sensemaking to describe how audiences develop emotional relationships with characters (Oatley 1999; Oatley and Gholamain 1997) may be more applicable to understanding emotional responses to the characters in Knockout Game and "happy slapping" videos than theories that are derived from fictional narrative-based formats. Retrospective sensemaking has seen widespread application in organizational communication contexts, yet this may be a prime opportunity for media effects research to explore its potential relevance and possibilities.

HOW REAL IS REAL?

Some of the most intriguing contributions of this project pertain to perceived realism assessments. It may seem counterintuitive to verify the realism of video footage of actual events. Yet the disengagement results, as well as the realism assessment item in post-viewing questionnaires, showed us that not everyone interprets realism in quite the same way. And later, we saw that providing pre-viewing information about the authenticity (or lack thereof) of the Knockout Game videos had no impact on the subjective evaluation of each individual viewer. People decided for themselves how real or not real this content was to them. Prior research in this area has also typically presented subjects with identical content tagged as either fictional or real. The well-supported Spinozan model posits that the comprehension and the acceptance of information occur simultaneously, following which some information may be tagged as unreliable and then discarded (Gilbert et al. 1990). This study made an interesting departure from this trend by providing subjects with real content and allowing *them* to decide how real it was. If the default processing mode is indeed to accept any and all information as real, surely the veracity of these video assaults should have never come into question in the first place. However, my participants' willingness to reject the realism of unambiguously *real* violence by drawing on coping and disengagement strategies poses an intriguing avenue for further investigation. When exactly during the comprehension process does information get tagged as fictional? Perhaps the overwhelmingly skeptical response to Clip 1 indicates an increasingly sophisticated and cynical media audience, quick to point out apparent inconsistencies and thereby avoid the discomfort and anxiety prompted by dysphoric content. This project demonstrates a promising future for the sustained analysis of the messy yet compelling relationships between disengagement, cognitive processing, and perceived realism.

On a more serious note, my results imply that the fictional world is increasingly becoming a standard whereby individuals evaluate and judge reality (Raney 2003). If true, this proposition has some staggering societal implications with regard to real-world attitudes and behavior. Raney observes that "if we can and are willing to stretch our real-world moral code for the sake of enjoyment, it seems reasonable to think that we can become conditioned to do so in real-world situations as well" (364). As real violence becomes increasingly prevalent in mainstream media outlets, audiences are becoming increasingly exposed to unfiltered images of fellow humans in graphically violent scenes. As technological developments facilitate a much higher level of media dependence—in corporate, informal, entertainment, information, and social networking contexts—than has previously existed, and media fragmentation betokens the burgeoning popularity of reality TV and web-based content, it is more important than ever that media effects research examines where exactly audiences draw the line between reality and fiction.

Some findings of this project also support research on how facts may be retained or discarded during the cognitive processing of information and perception of realism. Specifically, the fact that an attempt to "manipulate" and pre-define the authenticity of Knockout Game content did not succeed provides further evidence that realism may be a subjective and individual assessment, independent of pre-defined parameters (see Green and Brock 2000). Yet perceived realism research is beset by inherent challenges. Specifically, attempts to "tinker" with realism interfere with default realism processing, and run the risk of alerting participants of the researcher's goal. In other words, if I plan on investigating how exactly you make realism judgments in mundane everyday contexts, I want to observe your default realism assessment mode. The second that you notice or realize that you *are* evaluating realism, you pay more attention to it and this is no longer your default assessment process. If we were sitting on a park bench and a child with a green balloon ran past us, we might smile at the child's apparent pleasure. In those moments, the event has been seen and cognitively processed as real: we know that a child with a green balloon ran past as we sat on the park bench. But if I were to then turn to you and ask, "How convinced are you that a child with a balloon just ran in front of us?" I have now caused you to devote more cognitive focus to processing this information than before. Or again, if I told you beforehand, "In approximately ten seconds, a child with a green balloon will run past us," your cognitive response to this event when it occurs will be markedly different from if you had not been warned in advance. In other words, you are no longer assessing the realism of this event in quite the same way (your default mode) as if I had never interfered with your cognition in the first place.

Busselle et al. (2004) note that a viewer's default processing mode is to not evaluate the realism of a narrative unless prompted by some cue within the program or an external source, such as a researcher. Indeed, any attempt to manipulate realism prior to exposure interferes with the Spinozan model of comprehension (Gilbert et al. 1990), which posits the simultaneous comprehension and belief of information. Therefore, informing participants that the videos were real or staged may have spurred an uncommon interest in their content and simultaneously triggered an increased attention to detail and any apparent inconsistency. Prompting participants to ponder the realism of the video clips may have encouraged them to pay closer attention to their realism assessment process, and therefore encouraged atypical responses. This may also explain why some participants felt the urge to engage in critical counterargument or flat out rejection of the realism of these filmed assaults.

Despite these challenges, it is important for others to persist with investigations into how exactly we assess the realism of real media content, particularly if these assessments are likely to insulate us from caring about our fellow beings, and dissuade and hinder compassion for the pain and suffering of other people.

MEASURE FOR MEASURE

Perhaps one of the more indisputable concerns highlighted by this project is the scarcity—or indeed, absence—of appropriate instruments to accurately measure empathy and perceived realism for this media genre. The fact that a pre-existing Victim Evaluation questionnaire (Mullin and Linz 1995) had to be significantly altered and revamped indicates that empathic concern as an affective response toward media characters—and *real* media characters, in particular—has yet to receive sufficient and sustained scholarly attention. Existing empathic distress scales are primarily geared toward fictional content (de Wied et al. 1994) and contain items that are not relevant or applicable to real violence. In addition, items on these scales contain troubling wording that is likely to trigger "gendered" responses, such as "How congested was your nose?" and "Did you feel a lump in your throat?" (see de Wied et al. 1994). Questions such as these reflect that the questionnaire was clearly tailored to measure responses to the tearjerker fictional genre, where elaborate plot and character development facilitate such overwhelming physiological responses. Simultaneously, however, these items betray this questionnaire's complete lack of applicability and relevance to real media violence victims, such as those in the Knockout Game videos. It is very unlikely that shockingly brutal attacks that last barely half a minute could prompt similar physiological reactions to *Steel Magnolias* or *Terms of Endearment*. I therefore encourage researchers to move beyond conceptualizing empathy as a static and fixed emotional response that remains uniform across all contexts, and instead recognize that there are different strains of empathy. The empathy that one may feel for an elderly woman who is brutally beaten by teenage boys is qualitatively distinct from the empathy that one may experience for Allie and Noah in *The Notebook* or Hazel and Gus in *The Fault in Our Stars*. The sooner that media effects researchers acknowledge this distinction, the more likely that we will develop new instruments that accurately capture these distinctions and thus provide a more applicable indication of empathic concern for specific media characters. I suspect that an instrument designed to measure empathic concern for real media violence victims will benefit from less emotionally charged items.

We also observed how strong gender differences emerged when using trait-assessment instruments that contained suggestive gendered phrasing, yet these differences vanished when the same participants completed outcome measures devoid of emotionally charged and gender-evocative language. This demonstrates the danger of using self-assessment trait measures that reflect dominant cultural assumptions, because respondents may be motivated by an inner desire to self-identify with socially acceptable gender constructions and their accompanying cultural roles (Tajfel and Turner 1979). Research in other communication traditions has demonstrated a prevailing self-presentation bias (Heider 1958), in which evaluations of ourselves tend to be far more flattering and positive than may really be the case. It therefore behooves us to be more attentive to the language and wording of trait-assessment instruments, particularly when subsequent analysis indicates distinct and highly significant gender differences. In this case, the absence of parallel patterns in post-experiment responses set off warning bells, prompting me to take a closer look at why the pre- and post-test data results were so different. I encourage my colleagues to prudently and judiciously interpret data when it has been collected using scales that contain what may easily be construed as suggestive phraseology. Indeed, I strongly recommend modifying some existing trait measurement scales to minimize and avoid biased responses. Alternately, it may be advisable to tap into these self-assessments by consciously using neutral and other-centered language. For example, the post-experiment questionnaires used in these experiments measured empathic concern by way of *victim-centered* assessments, rather than evaluations of the self. Removing or minimizing the need to implicate oneself in these research instruments may elicit more honest and candid responses from participants, untainted by the (quite possibly unintentional) motivation to paint a flattering self-image.

On a related note, the study that focused specifically on gender differences (see chapter 7) further corroborates recent investigations that emphasize individual differences—rather than broad demographic categories—in how we respond to media stimuli (Nabi and Riddle 2008; Oliver et al. 2009). Personality trait variables such as empathy, sensation seeking, neuroticism, and extraversion and may be better indicators of human thought and behavior than demographic groupings based on gender, age, and ethnicity. In fact, significant associations that do emerge when these broad demographic labels are employed may actually be the result of several interacting trait variables for which the larger demographic identifier (gender, in this case) serves as a marker. The results of this research study make a strong argument for individual differences by determining no significant responses between male and female viewers' affective responses to real media violence. Accordingly, I urge my fellow media effects researchers (if they are not already doing so) to strongly consider focusing on individual differences stemming from personality attributes rather than pigeonholing participants solely on the basis of broad demographic categories.

This chapter has summarized a few of the theoretical contributions that this research project offers existing paradigms. Yet theoretical application and extension is but one half of that all-important "so what" factor. The more pragmatic and utilitarian contributions of this project pertain to its implications for society as a whole.

NINE

Why We Should Care

Most of the students who participated in this project, showed up, completed the experiment, and made sure that I had all the information to ensure that they would receive course-related extra credit for completing this requirement. And then, obligatory research participation over and done with, they were gone. In general, my attempts to clarify any questions about the research or the videos were met with polite refusals and shakes of the head, as they hurried off to other pre-existing appointments. Occasionally, however, participation in my research prompted wonderful and insightful conversations with those who were brimming over with questions and observations about their experience. What exactly, they wondered, was I trying to investigate? How were their responses to the online survey from two weeks ago related to these new questionnaires? Sometimes, they just wanted to chat about the Knockout Game videos that they had watched. I recall one such conversation with a college junior named Josh. As he finished the last questionnaire and then collected his backpack to leave, Josh appeared pensive. As I prepared to recite the usual perfunctory statements expressing gratitude and offering to clarify any lingering questions, Josh spoke first. "That was unreal," he paused. "Where did you find that stuff?" An interesting discussion ensued about "happy slapping" and Knockout Game videos, as we chatted about the increasing availability online, and why anyone might desire to record these horrific assaults, let alone commit them. "You don't see a lot of this on TV," said Josh, "but it's out there. I've seen stuff like this online. And worse." He's right, of course. We live in an age of unprecedented digital connectedness, in which the slightest phrase, image, meme, or video has the potential to go viral in seconds, eliciting instant mass audiences.

At approximately 2:00 a.m. on January 1, 2009, Oscar Grant and his friends were on their way back from a New Year's Eve night of revelry, when they were pulled from their train at an Oakland station by Bay Area Rapid Transit police officers. In the ensuing commotion as the officers attempted to restrain the young men, Grant was pressed facedown onto the platform. Suddenly, and with no apparent provocation, BART Officer Johannes Mehserle stood over Grant and fired a bullet into his lower back that ricocheted off the platform and punctured Grant's lung, killing him within minutes. This incident would have gone largely unnoticed had it not been for the other passengers on the waiting train, who seized their cellphones and recorded the event (Antony and Thomas 2010). Although BART officers soon tried to confiscate all footage of the shooting, some passengers had the presence of mind to hide their phones. Multiple videos of the shooting were posted on YouTube within days (Egelko 2009). The primary raw footage of this incident is still available on YouTube as I write these words, and has accumulated 1,438,716 total views since it was posted (*Los Angeles Times*, June 24, 2010).

In September 2009, sixteen-year-old honor student Derrion Albert's brutal beating and death at the hands of classmates was captured on cellphone video and distributed across the Internet (Martinez, September 29, 2009). This video is still available online and currently registers 133,661 views (P4CM, October 3, 2009).

In September 2012, an American Border Patrol agent shot and killed a Mexican man on the Mexican side of the border. Again, the incident was recorded by others on their cellphones and later posted online. At the time of writing, this video is still available and has 24,401 views on YouTube (*David Pakman Show*, September 14, 2012).

On the off chance that you are tempted to dismiss these incidents as sporadic instances of filmed assaults, allow me to present two events that occurred over the span of a single week. In retaliation against the alleged execution of three Israeli teenagers, Israeli police were caught on cellphone cameras viciously kicking and brutalizing a young Palestinian boy. The video is available on YouTube and drew 30,772 views over just six days (*Geo News*, July 5, 2014). A day earlier, travelers on a California highway captured a cellphone video of a California Highway Patrol officer astride an elderly woman whom he had pulled from her vehicle, in the act of savagely and repeatedly punching her in the head. This video is also still available on YouTube and amassed 223,935 views over barely seven days (YouWatchMedia, July 4, 2014).

Incidentally, the number of views reported for each of these videos is indicative only of how many times they have been played on YouTube alone. Their exposure was significantly amplified by subsequent mainstream mass media coverage. As a result of the attention that these preceding incidents gained after the videos went viral online, all these stories—and the accompanying original cellphone footage of these often fatal attacks—were featured on national cable news channels. Sadly, major cable channels sometimes unintentionally capture and disseminate graphic violent images themselves. Such was the case when *Fox News* screened live images of a high-speed police chase. The production staff and news anchors were caught entirely unprepared when the pursued suspect abandoned his vehicle to run a short distance and then fatally shoot himself in the head. The news anchor covering this developing story, Shepard Smith, was compelled to offer an instant apology for the network's lapse in unintentionally exposing millions of viewers to this horrific incident. The original unsettling video is still available on YouTube as I write this, and has garnered 296,720 views since it was first posted online (DubbsProductions, September 28, 2012).

Audiences today are confronted with an abundance of violent images distributed throughout broadcast media, including online videos posted on popular video sharing websites. Increasingly, much of this content features *real* people in violent situations. Recent grotesque propaganda videos of American, British, and French hostages being beheaded by Islamic fundamentalist groups received widespread media coverage and public condemnation (Callimachi and de Freytas-Tamura, October 3, 2014). Countless disturbing videos of executions, mutilations, torture, and other atrocities perpetrated by the terrorist group ISIS have been released on public online portals such as YouTube—with the sole disclaimer "Graphic Content"—have accumulated millions of hits (or views) since they were posted barely a few months ago.

In each of the preceding instances, average viewers could watch raw online footage of a fellow human suffer horrific injuries, and sometimes fatally succumb to these attacks. Anyone—I mean, *anyone*—can access and watch these videos. It is important to remember that there is no current way of restricting this content or making it entirely inaccessible to younger impressionable viewers. Although some of these videos are prefaced by an advisory message that warns of explicit content, YouTube users need merely click on a button to verify that they are above eighteen years of age—hardly a strong deterrent for a curious young viewer. More recently, some websites require users to sign in before they watch graphic or disturbing content. Yet even this is apparent obstacle is easily overcome by determined and inquisitive users who can quickly create the false credentials that then permit them to watch real media violence. Additionally, sites such as YouTube have no feasible process of combing through the millions of videos posted online, let alone the thousands of new ones that are added every day. Instead, they rely on a form of crowd policing, where users can "flag" content that they consider disturbing or otherwise inappropriate. If enough users complain, the content is pulled off the site. But not before a staggering number of viewers have already seen it, particularly if the video first went viral.

In light of this increasing availability and accessibility to graphic real violence online, my research offers a timely and valuable insight into how audiences respond to this subgenre of user-generated real media violence. Although the Knockout Game and "happy slapping" videos do not share the exact characteristics of the violent depictions in some of the videos described above, there are undoubtedly some common features. All these videos capture severe physical injury inflicted on another human being. Whether we are compelled to watch out of sweeping compassion or morbid fascination, the unspeakable brutality of these images necessarily impacts our cognitive and affective responses to this content. The main distinction between Knockout Game videos and other surveillance footage of real attacks is that the former are recorded and distributed by the attackers themselves, or by someone closely associated with the attackers. But does this in any way diminish the intensity or savagery of the onscreen violence? Does it imply that the victim fared better in one instance rather than the other? The terrible videos released by ISIS also serve as similar "trophies" of war, capturing real world atrocities so that they may be strategically disseminated online. Is there a qualitative distinction in our likely affective responses to these different categories of real media violence?

Although my specific intent was to research how audiences emotionally respond to Knockout Game videos, I take this opportunity to remind readers that at no point were my participants informed that these were specifically Knockout Game videos prior to participation. In the absence of this contextualizing framework, they received no preface or advance warning to prepare them for the content prior to watching random assaults on unsuspecting victims. Yet, we witnessed several ways in which people creatively dismissed or rejected the evident pain and suffering of another human being. Blaming the victim, the context, and production aesthetics, viewers found ways to insulate themselves from feeling concern and empathy for these victims. Even though some participants did report high empathic concern, it is nevertheless disheartening that these responses constituted the minority. This may portend a new kind of desensitization, an emotional deadening of sorts, that goes well beyond audiences' appetites for ever more graphic and explicit (fictional) content. Indeed, the preponderance of increasingly vivid brutality and gorgeous spectacle that has come to characterize what we now expect from movies and television may be reconfiguring our fictional schemata about *what* exactly constitutes violence—its very nature and essence. Ultimately, the distant and blurred image of a young boy being kicked by military police seems relatively tame compared to gushing carotid arteries and splintering bones. Even in the most intimate Knockout Game videos, we are never quite that close to the action.

Yet real violence is scary and disturbing primarily because of its unpredictable and chaotic nature. In the wake of mass shootings and terrible accidents, we struggle to make sense of these events by attempting to organize details and assign meaning and structure to something that defies understanding. Who was this person, and why did they commit such horrific crimes? Accessible and trite schemata inevitably rise to the surface, enabling us to sort through the mess of emerging facts, and thus identify those all-important details that allow us to tame the terrifying and unfamiliar. Yet, if nothing else, it is my hope that this project has demonstrated the danger of applying fictional schematas to real-world violence and its victims. This is because relying on these filmic narrative-based mental frameworks encourages the primarily passive consumption and aesthetic distance that we have learned to cultivate with media narratives and characters, and extends this passive spectatorship to real life and actual events. Concern and empathic distress for these victims of violence are reduced to a pale shadow of the original sentiment—much like our diluted and transient emotional responses toward fictional media characters that fade and dissipate at the narrative's conclusion.

If current trends are any indication, the prevalence of real media violence looks set to increase exponentially over coming years. Particularly with the advent of increasingly sophisticated smart devices, enabled with powerful high-resolution cameras, anyone anywhere can record whatever they like and instantly share it online. Images of playful pets chasing their tails vie with videos of bullying and victimization for our attention. The growing popularity of wearable technology, such as Google Glass and other similar devices, heralds a new era of video surveillance and production where cameras have the ability to intrude into and capture increasingly private and confidential content. We are already beginning to see the implications of these technological developments with regard to an intrepid breed of citizen journalists, determined to "expose" even the riskiest situations to mass digital audiences. Disturbing videos of military suppression and torture in repressive regimes that would previously never have been accessible are now posted on social networking websites and broadcast beyond physical borders. Websites such as Liveleak.com and VICE News offer uncensored and unfiltered images directly from warzones and disaster-struck areas.

In the wake of this escalating availability to real media violence, is it important for us to retain the vestiges of our humanity and still care for another person's pain and injury? Will we balk in the face of actual brutalities, and find ways to erect physical and mental barriers that shield us from emotional anxiety and psychological discomfort? Do we have the courage to confront the cruelties of this world, as well as the cognitive coping strategies that we use to dismiss them? Do we dare to care? It is my fervent hope that we do, because only if we are willing to challenge reality can we hope to change it. As noted by psychotherapist Nathaniel Branden, "The first step toward change is awareness. The second step is acceptance" (2014).

Appendix A

Research Instruments

1. Trait Empathy

   <u>Empathic Concern</u>

   a. When I see someone being taken advantage of, I feel kind of protective toward them.
   b. When I see someone being treated unfairly, I sometimes don't feel very much pity for them. (Reverse Coded)
   c. I often have tender, concerned feelings for people less fortunate than me.
   d. I would describe myself as a pretty soft-hearted person.
   e. Sometimes I don't feel sorry for other people when they are having problems. (Reverse Coded)
   f. Other people's misfortunes do not usually disturb me a great deal. (Reverse Coded)
   g. I am often quite touched by things that I see happen.

   <u>Personal Distress Scale</u>

   a. When I see someone who badly needs help in an emergency, I go to pieces.
   b. I sometimes feel helpless when I am in the middle of a very emotional situation.
   c. In emergency situations, I feel apprehensive and ill-at-ease.
   d. I am usually pretty effective in dealing with emergencies. (Reverse Coded)
   e. Being in a tense emotional situation scares me.
   f. When I see someone get hurt, I tend to remain calm. (Reverse Coded)
   g. I tend to lose control during emergencies.

2. Empathic Distress: Modified Victim Evaluation Questionnaire

   <u>Victim Sympathy</u>

   a. I feel sympathy for the victim.
   b. I feel pity for the victim.

    c. I feel sorry for the victim.
    d. Do you think the victim was treated unjustly?

Victim Injury
Do you think that:

    a. the victim might need psychological help as a result of being assaulted?
    b. the victim might have suffered psychological damage because of the assault?
    c. there will be any lasting negative impact from the attack?
    d. the victim might suffer short-term physical harm as a result of the assault?
    e. the victim might suffer long-term physical injury from the attack?
    f. the attacker should receive some form of punishment?

3. Victim complicity
   Do you think that:

    a. the victim knew his attacker(s)?
    b. he knew in advance that he was going to be attacked?
    c. he was a willing participant in the attack?

4. Trait Enjoyment of Media Violence

    a. I enjoy TV shows more if they have lots of excitement, like fights and explosions.
    b. As far as I am concerned, the more violent a TV show is, the better.

5. Enjoyment of the Video Clip

    a. I liked the clip very much.
    b. The clip was exciting.
    c. The clip was enjoyable.
    d. I would like to watch more videos like this.

6. Perceived Realism
   Based on your responses to the previous [Victim Complicity] question, do you think that this video clip was:

    a. Totally fake
    b. Fake
    c. Somewhat fake
    d. Somewhat real
    e. Real
    f. Totally real

7. Familiarity

     a. Have you seen this video clip before?

8. Demographic Information

    Age, Gender, Ethnicity

Appendix B

Post-Test Questionnaire

1. Empathic distress: Modified Victim Evaluation Questionnaire

   Victim Sympathy

      a. I feel sympathy for the victim.
      b. I feel pity for the victim.
      c. I feel sorry for the victim.
      d. Do you think the victim was treated unjustly?

   Victim Injury
   Do you think that:

      a. the victim might need psychological help as a result of being assaulted?
      b. the victim might have suffered psychological damage because of the assault?
      c. there will be any lasting negative impact from the attack?
      d. the victim might suffer short-term physical harm as a result of the assault?
      e. the victim might suffer long-term physical injury from the attack?
      f. the attacker should receive some form of punishment?

2. Have you seen this video clip before?
3. Perceived Realism of the Attack:
   Do you think that:

      a. the victim knew his attacker(s)?
      b. he knew in advance that he was going to be attacked?
      c. he was a willing participant in the attack?
      d. Based on your previous responses, do you think that this video clip was:

         • Totally fake
         • Fake
         • Somewhat fake
         • Somewhat real

- Real
- Totally real

Bibliography

Antony, M. G., and R. J. Thomas. (2010). "'This is Citizen Journalism at Its Finest': YouTube and the Public Sphere in the Oscar Grant Shooting Incident." *New Media & Society 12*(8), 1280–1296.

Aquino, K., A. Reed II, S. Thau, and D. Freeman. (2006). "A Grotesque and Dark Beauty: How Moral Identity and Mechanisms of Moral Disengagement Influence Cognitive and Emotional Reactions to War." *Journal of Experimental Social Psychology 43*(3), 385–92.

Bandura, A. (1965). "Vicarious Processes: A Case of No-Trial Learning." *Advances in Experimental Social Psychology 2*, 1–55.

Bandura, A. (1999). "Moral Disengagement in the Perpetration of Inhumanities." *Personality and Social Psychology Review 3*(3), 193–209.

Bandura, A. (2001). "Social Cognitive Theory of Mass Communication." *Media Psychology 3*, 265–299.

Bandura, A. (2002). "Selective Moral Disengagement in the Exercise of Moral Agency." *Journal of Moral Education 31*, 101–119.

Bandura, A. (2007). "Social Cognitive Theory." In R. T. Craig and H. L. Muller (eds.), *Theorizing Communication: Readings Across Traditions*, 339–356. Los Angeles: Sage Publications.

Bandura, A., Barbaranelli, C., Caprara, G. V., and C. Pastorelli. (1996). "Mechanisms of Moral Disengagement in the Exercise of Moral Agency." *Journal of Personality and Social Psychology 71* (2), 364–374.

Berkowitz, L., and J. T. Alioto. (1973). "The Meaning of an Observed Event as a Determinant of Its Aggressive Consequences." *Journal of Personality and Social Psychology 28*(2), 206–217.

Branden, N. (2014). "Nathaniel Branden quotes." ThinkExist.com. Retrieved 07/05/2014, thinkexist.com/quotation/the_first_step_toward_change_is_awareness-the/217206.html.

Bruce, L. (1995). "At the Intersection of Real-Life and Television Violence: Emotional Effects, Cognitive Effects, and Interpretive Activities of Children." Unpublished doctoral dissertation, University of Wisconsin–Madison.

Bryant, J., and S. Thompson. (2002). *Fundamentals of Media Effects*. New York: McGraw Hill.

Buckley, C. (2013, November 22). "Police Unsure if Random Attacks Are Rising Threat or Urban Myth." *The New York Times*, A19.

Busselle, R., and H. Bilandzic. (2008). "Fictionality and Perceived Realism in Experiencing Stories: A Model of Narrative Comprehension and Engagement." *Communication Theory 18*, 255–280.

Busselle, R., A. Ryabovolova, and B. Wilson. (2004). "Ruining a Good Story: Cultivation, Perceived Realism and Narrative." *Communications 29*, 365–378.

Callimachi, R., and K. de Freytas-Tamura. (2014, October 3). "ISIS Releases Video of Execution of British Aid Worker." *The New York Times*, A6.

Cantor, J. (1998). "Children's Attraction to Violent Television Programming." In J. Goldstein (ed.), *Why We Watch: The Attractions of Violent Entertainment*, 88–115. New York: Oxford University Press.

Cantor, J. (2002). "Fright Reactions to Mass Media." In J. Bryant and D. Zillman (eds.), *Media Effects: Advances in Theory and Research*, 287–306. New Jersey: Lawrence Erlbaum.

Carroll, N. (1997). "Art, Narrative, and Emotion." In M. Hjort and S. Laver (eds.), *Emotion and the Arts*, 190–211. New York: Oxford University Press.

Cohen, J. (2001). "Defining Identification: A Theoretical Look at the Identification of Audiences with Media Characters." *Mass Communication & Society 4*(3), 245–264.

David Pakman Show (2012, September 14). "Border Patrol Agent Shoots across Border, Kills Mexican Man." Retrieved 07/11/2014, www.youtube.com/watch?v=G6BlfAwc0jQ.

Davis, M. H. (1980). "A Multi-Dimensional Approach to Individual Differences in Empathy." *JSAS Catalog of Selected Documents in Psychology 10*, 85–102.

de Wied, M., D. Zillmann, and V. Ordman. (1994). "The Role of Empathic Distress in the Enjoyment of Cinematic Tragedy." *Poetics 23*, 91–106.

de Zúñigal, H. G., N. Jung, and S. Valenzuela. (2012). "Social Media Use for News and Individuals' Social Capital, Civic Engagement and Political Participation." *Journal of Computer-Mediated Communication 17*(3), 319–36.

Demby, G. (2013, November 27). "'The Knockout Game': An Old Phenomenon With Fresh Branding." *NPR: Code Switch*. Retrieved 12/28/2013, www.npr.org/blogs/codeswitch/2013/11/27/247366898/the-knockout-game-an-old-phenomenon-with-fresh-branding.

Detert, J. R., Trevino, L. K., and V. L. Sweitzer. (2008). "Moral Disengagement in Ethical Decision Making: A Study of Antecedents and Outcomes." *Journal of Applied Psychology 93*(2), 374–391.

DubbsProductions (2012, September 28). "Man Shoots Himself on Fox News (Graphic)." Retrieved 07/11/2014, www.youtube.com/watch?v=oOMcbd7acMM.

Egelko, B. (2009). "BART Shooting Draws Rodney King Case Parallels." *San Francisco Chronicle* (15 January): A1.

Eyrich, N., M. L. Padman, and K. D. Sweetser. (2008). "PR Practitioners' Use of Social Media Tools and Communication Technology." *Public Relations Review 34*(4), 412–14.

Geo News 2014 (2014, July 5). "Israeli Soldiers Beating a Palestinian Boy in Palestine-Israel Army Brutality." Retrieved 07/11/2014, www.youtube.com/watch?v=blGcylUXNVE.

Gerbner, G., L. Gross, N. Signorielli, and M. Morgan. (1980). "Television Violence, Victimization, and Power." *The American Behavioral Scientist 23*(5), 705–716.

Gerrig, R. J. (1993). *Experiencing Narrative Worlds: On the Psychological Activities of Reading*. New Haven, CT: Yale University Press.

Gilbert, D. T., D. S. Krull, and P. S. Malone. (1990). "Unbelieving the Unbelievable: Some Problems in the Rejection of False Information." *Journal of Personality and Social Psychology 59*(4), 601–613.

Goldstein, J. (1998). "Why We Watch." In J. Goldstein (ed.), *Why We Watch: The Attractions of Violent Entertainment*, 212–226. New York: Oxford University Press.

Green, M. C. (2004). "Transportation into Narrative Worlds: The Role of Prior Knowledge in Perceived Realism." *Discourse Processes 38*(2), 247–266.

Green, M. C., and T. C. Brock. (2000). "The Role of Transportation in the Persuasiveness of Public Narratives." *Journal of Personality and Social Psychology 79*(5), 701–721.

Guttman, A. (1998). "The Appeal of Violent Sports." In J. Goldstein (ed.), *Why We Watch: The Attractions of Violent Entertainment*, 7–26. New York: Oxford University Press.

Hall, A. (2003). "Reading Realism: Audiences' Evaluations of the Reality of Media Texts." *Journal of Communication 53*(4), 624–641.

Haridakis, P., and G. Hanson. (2009). "Social Interaction and Co-Viewing with YouTube: Blending Mass Communication Reception and Social Connection." *Journal of Broadcasting & Electronic Media 53*(2), 317–35.

Hartmann, T., and P. Vorderer. (2009). "It's Okay to Shoot a Character: Moral Disengagement in Violent Video Games." *Journal of Communication 60*(1), 94–119.

Hatfield, E., J. T. Cacioppo, and R. L. Rapson. (1994). *Emotional Contagion*. New York: Cambridge University Press.

Heider, F. (1958). *The Psychology of Interpersonal Relations.* New York: John Wiley & Sons.

Hoffner, C., and J. Cantor, J. (1991). "Perceiving and Responding to Mass Media Characters." In J. Bryant and D. Zillmann (eds.), *Responding to the Screen: Reception and Reaction Processes,* 63–101. New Jersey: Lawrence Erlbaum Associates.

Honigsbaum, M. (2005). "Concern Over Rise of 'Happy Slapping' Craze." *The Guardian.* Retrieved on April 26, 2007, from www.guardian.co.uk/mobile/article/ 0,2763,1470214,00.html.

Jonsson, P. (2013, December 27). "White Man Charged with 'Knockout Game' Hate Crime. Racial Hypocrisy?" *The Christian Science Monitor: Justice.* Retrieved 12/28/ 2013, www.csmonitor.com/USA/Justice/2013/1227/White-man-charged-with-knockout-game-hate-crime.-Racial-hypocrisy.

Konijn, E. A., and J. F. Hoorn. (2005). "Some Like it Bad: Testing a Model for Perceiving and Experiencing Fictional Characters." *Media Psychology 7,* 107-144.

Krakowiak, K. M., and M. Tsay. (2011). "The Role of Moral Disengagement in the Enjoyment of Real and Fictional Characters." *International Journal of Arts and Technology 4*(1), 90–101.

Lachlan, K. A., and R. Tamborini. (2008). "The Effect of Perpetrator Motive and Dispositional Attributes on Enjoyment of Television Violence and Attitudes toward Victims." *Journal of Broadcasting & Electronic Media 52*(1), 136–152.

Levinson, J. (1997). "Emotion in Response to Art: A Survey of the Terrain." In M. Hjort and S. Laver (eds.), *Emotion and the Arts,* 20–36. New York: Oxford University Press.

Lindlof, T. R., and B. C. Taylor. (2002). *Qualitative Communication Research Methods.* Thousand Oaks, CA: Sage.

Los Angeles Times (2010, June 24). "Court Releases Dramatic Video of BART Shooting." Los Angeles Times: Official YouTube channel. Retrieved 07/11/2014, www.youtube.com/watch?v=Q2LDw5l_yMI.

Martinez, E. (2009, September 29). "Photos: Derrion Albert Uncut Beating Death Video." CBSNews.com. Retrieved 06/10/2009, www.cbsnews.com/8301-504083_162-5350883-504083.html.

Maslin, J. (2014). "*Fargo* (1996): Overview." *The New York Times*: Movies. Retrieved 05/ 26/2014, www.nytimes.com/movies/movie/135867/Fargo/overview.

McAllister, A. L., A. Bandura, T. C. Morrison, and J. Gussendorf. (2003). "Mechanisms of Moral Disengagement in Support of Military Force: The Impact of 9/11." Unpublished manuscript.

McCauley, C. (1998). "When Screen Violence is not Attractive." In J. Goldstein (ed.), *Why We Watch: The Attractions of Violent Entertainment,* 144–162. New York: Oxford University Press.

Mendelsohn, A. L., and Z. Papacharissi. (2007). "Reality vs. Fiction: How Defined Realness affects Cognitive and Emotional Responses to Photographs." *Visual Communication Quarterly 14,* 231–243.

Moore, C. (2008). "Moral Disengagement in Processes of Organizational Corruption." *Journal of Business Ethics 80*(1), 129–139.

Mullin, C. R., and D. Linz. (1995). "Desensitization and Resensitization to Violence against Women: Effects of Exposure to Sexually Violent Films on Judgments of Domestic Violence Victims." *Journal of Personality and Social Psychology 69* (3), 449–459.

Nabi, R. L., and K. Riddle. (2008). "Personality Traits, Television Viewing, and the Cultivation Effect." *Journal of Broadcasting & Electronic Media 52*(3), 327–348.

Oatley, K. (1999). "Meeting of Minds: Dialogue, Sympathy, and Identification in Reading Fiction." *Poetics 26,* 439–454.

Oatley, K., and M. Gholamain. (1997). "Emotions and Identification: Connections between Readers and Fiction." In M. Hjort and S. Laver (eds.), *Emotion and the Arts,* 263–281. New York: Oxford University Press.

Oliver, M. B. (1993). "Exploring the Paradox of the Enjoyment of Sad Films." *Human Communication Research 19*(3), 315–342.

Oliver, M. B. (1996). "Influences of Authoritarianism and Portrayals of Race on Caucasian Viewers' Responses to Reality-Based Crime Dramas." *Communication Reports 9*, 141–150.

Oliver, M. B., and K. M. Krakowiak. (2009). "When Good Characters Do Bad Things: Examining the Effect of Moral Ambiguity on Enjoyment." Paper presented at the Association for Education in Journalism and Mass Communication convention, August 5–8, 2009, Boston.

Osborn, B. (1993). "Beyond Blame: Media Literacy as Violence Prevention. Media and Violence: Making the Connection." *Media & Values 62*. Retrieved 06/10/2014, www.medialit.org/reading-room/violence-formula-analyzing-tv-video-and-movies.

Osofsky, M. J., Bandura, A., and P. G. Zimbardo. (2005). "The Role of Moral Disengagement in the Execution Process." *Law and Human Behavior 29*(4), 371–393.

Oxford Dictionaries (2014). "Slaphappy: Definition." Oxford Dictionaires.com. Retrieved 06/13/2014, www.oxforddictionaries.com/us/definition/american_english/slaphappy.

P4CM (2009, October 3). "Raw video of Teen beat to death (Derrion Albert)." Retrieved 10/29/2014, www.youtube.com/watch?v=Hdk9Ys_lVdw.

Pelton, J., Gound, M., Forehand, R., and G. Brody. (2004). "The Moral Disengagement Scale: Extension with an American Minority Sample." *Journal of Psychopathology and Behavioral Assessment 26*(1), 31–39.

Pouliot, L., and P. S. Cowen. (2007). "Does Perceived Realism Really Matter in Media Effects?" *Media Psychology 9*(2), 241–259.

Raacke, J., and J. Bonds-Raacke. (2008). "Myspace and Facebook: Applying the Uses and Gratifications Theory to Exploring Friend-Networking Sites." *CyberPsychology & Behavior 11*(2), 169–174.

Raney, A. A. (2003). "Disposition-Based Theories of Enjoyment." In J. Bryant, J. Cantor, and D. Roskos-Ewoldsen (eds.), *Communication and Emotions: Essays in Honor of Dolf Zillmann*, 61–84. Mahwah, NJ: Erlbaum.

Raney, A. A. (2006). "The Psychology of Disposition-Based Theories of Media Enjoyment." In J. Bryant and P. Vorderer (eds.), *Psychology of Entertainment*, 137–150. New Jersey: Lawrence Erlbaum.

Raney, A. A., and J. Bryant. (2002). "Moral Judgment and Crime Drama: An Integrated Theory of Enjoyment." *Journal of Communication 52*, 402–415.

Raney, A. A., H. Schmid, J. Niemann, and M. Ellensohn. (2009). "Testing Affective Disposition Theory: A Comparison of the Enjoyment of Hero and Antihero Narratives." Paper presented at the 59th annual meeting of the International Communication Association, May 21–25, 2009, Chicago.

Richmond, J., and J. C. Wilson. (2008). "Are Graphic Media Violence, Aggression and Moral Disengagement Related?" *Psychiatry, Psychology and Law 15*(2), 350–57.

Riddle, K., K. Eyal, C. Mahood, and W. J. Potter. (2006). "Judging the Degree of Violence in Media Portrayals: A Cross-Genre Comparison." *Journal of Broadcasting & Electronic Media 50*(2), 270–286.

Rossen, J., and A. Patel. (2013, November 25). "'Knockout Game': Teens Attack Innocent People just for Fun." *Today News*. Retrieved 06/14/2014, www.today.com/news/knockout-game-teens-attack-innocent-people-just-fun-2D11648773.

Shafer, D. M., and A. A. Raney. (2012). "Exploring How We Enjoy Antihero Narratives." *Journal of Communication 62*(6), 1028–1046.

Strauss, A., and J. Corbin. (1998). *Basics of Qualitative Research*. Thousand Oaks, CA: Sage.

Tajfel, H., and J. Turner. (1979). "An Integrative Theory of Intergroup Conflict." In W. G. Austin and S. Worchel (eds.), *The Social Psychology of Intergroup Relations*, 94–109. Monterey, CA: Brooks-Cole.

Tamborini, R., A. Eden, N. D. Bowman, M. Grizzard, and K. Lachlan. (2009). "The Influence of Morality Subcultures on the Acceptance and Appeal of Violence."

Paper presented at the 59th annual meeting of the International Communication Association, May 21–25, 2009, Chicago.

Tannenbaum, P. H. (1980). "Entertainment as Vicarious Emotional Experience." In P. H. Tannenbaum (ed.), *The Entertainment Functions of Television*, 107–129. New Jersey: Lawrence Erlbaum.

Vollum, S., J. Buffington-Vollum, and D. R. Longmire. (2004). "Moral Disengagement and Attitudes about Violence toward Animals." *Society & Animals* 12(3), 209–235.

Vorderer, P., C. Klimmt, and U. Ritterfeld. (2004). "Enjoyment: At the Heart of Media Entertainment." *Communication Theory* 14(4), 388–408.

Walsh, M. (2014, October 22). "Psychiatrists Disagree over Second Slender Man Stabbing Suspect's Mental State." *New York Daily News*. Retrieved 10/25/2014, www.nydailynews.com/news/crime/psychiatrists-disagree-slender-man-stabbing-suspect-mental-state-article-1.1983168.

YouWatchMedia (2014, July 04). "VIDEO - California Highway Patrol Officer Beating Woman in the Head on Side of Road." Retrieved 07/11/2014, www.youtube.com/watch?v=NV7lO_1kWfo.

Zillmann, D. (1991). "Empathy: Affect from Bearing Witness to the Emotions of Others." In J. Bryant and D. Zillmann (eds.), *Responding to the Screen: Reception and Reaction Processes*, 135–167. New Jersey: Lawrence Erlbaum.

Zillmann, D. (1994). "Mechanisms of Emotional Involvement with Drama." *Poetics* 23, 33–51.

Zillmann, D., and J. R. Cantor. (1976). "A Disposition Theory of Humour and Mirth." In A. J. Chapman and H. C. Foot (eds.), *Humor and Laughter: Theory, Research, and Applications*, 93–115. Piscataway, NJ: Transaction Publishers.

Zillmann, D., and S. Knobloch. (2001). "Emotional Reactions to Narratives about the Fortunes of Personae in the News Theater." *Poetics* 29, 189–206.

Index

affective disposition theory, 18–20, 84, 109–111; retrospective sensemaking versus, 85, 111

Bandura, Albert, 23–24, 28, 48, 54, 55, 57, 61, 68, 107

cellphone video, 5, 6, 9, 44–45, 47, 50, 62, 68, 118–119; YouTube and viral videos, 2, 8, 9, 44, 50, 52, 76, 93, 118–119
cognitive coping mechanisms, 3, 8, 29–31, 35, 48, 49, 54, 68, 106, 121
cognitive coping strategies. *See* cognitive coping mechanisms

desensitization, 8–9, 14, 27, 35, 44, 56, 72, 104, 107, 120

emotion, 12, 91; media characters and, 18, 20, 22; narratives and, 11. *See also* affective disposition theory
empathic concern. *See* empathic distress
empathic distress, 20, 22, 74, 77, 80–81, 84–85, 93, 94, 95–96, 98–100, 114; gender, 90–92, 95–97, 98–100, 114; group viewing contexts, 74–75, 105; individual differences versus, 50, 91, 97, 115; measurement, 40–41; trait empathy, 21, 93, 94, 96, 98–100, 114
empathy, 1, 17, 39–41, 90–92, 114; affective disposition theory and, 18
"happy slapping", 6–7, 7, 9, 25, 35, 47–48. *See also* Knockout Game

Knockout Game, 2, 7–8, 25, 48, 86, 110, 120; empathic distress and, 20–21; media enjoyment, 18, 43, 93, 94;

moral disengagement and, 31–32; realism, 61–67; video selection, 44–46, 50–52, 76; violence and, 43, 48, 90, 93, 94, 96–97

media violence, 1–2, 7–9, 27; genuine versus fake, 49, 53, 68; real media violence, 10, 33–35, 48, 68, 106, 111, 117–121
moral disengagement, 3, 24, 32, 48, 106–108; advantageous comparison, 25; attributive blame, 28, 55, 56, 68, 107; dehumanization, 27–28; diffusion of responsibility, 26; displacement of responsibility, 25; euphemistic labeling, 25; logical inconsistency, 57–58, 68, 107; minimizing consequences, 26, 55, 56, 68, 107; moral justification, 24

normalized social deviance, 66–67, 68, 108

perceived realism, 16, 43–44, 54, 68, 77–86, 112–114; Cartesian model, 14–15; pre-viewing disclaimer and, 71–72, 74, 75, 78–81, 85–86, 113; real versus fictional information, 14–16, 73, 111–113; Spinozan model, 15–16, 73, 74, 85, 112, 113
premeditated prank, 59–61, 68. *See also* victim complicity

schema, 13–14, 31, 58, 63–64, 68, 109, 111, 121

user-generated content, 2, 9, 104

victim responsibility, 40–41, 42. *See also* victim complicity

135

About the Author

Mary Grace Antony, PhD, is assistant professor of communication studies at Schreiner University. Her research encompasses media studies, audience discourse, globalization, and new media technology. When she is not conducting research, grading assignments, or teaching, she enjoys watching movies, experimenting in the kitchen, and hiking in the Texas Hill Country with her husband and dog.